ANGEL IN A TENT

Heeding To The Call

Saundra Mills

authorHOUSE®

AuthorHouse™
1663 Liberty Drive
Bloomington, IN 47403
www.authorhouse.com
Phone: 1-800-839-8640

First published by AuthorHouse   7/28/2010

ISBN: 978-1-4520-3281-8 (sc)

Printed in the United States of America
Bloomington, Indiana

This book is printed on acid-free paper.

Angel In A Tent

He who conceals his sins
Does not prosper, but whoever
Confesses and renounces them
Finds Mercy.

Proverb 28:13

DEDICATION

This book is dedicated to my Lord and Savior Yashua Jesus the Christ. Who is my first love, and without him I am nothing.

Second I would like to dedicate this book and thank my Mother Lessie, who is a woman of God. She has been the strength of the Family. Her kindness to others goes a long way, and without her I would Not be here today writing this book.

Third I would like to dedicate this book to my daughter Makele, who is a mini me. Makele has brought joy into my life. She is a Beautiful young lady who has beautiful talents that God has blessed her With. I say this to you Makele, never give up on your dreams. Always Continue to stay focused on those dreams, put God first in everything. Stay Surrounded with positive people. I Love You so much.

Fourth I would like to Thank God for placing this special Man in my life. I dedicate this book to my husband Robert. You are a kind Loveable person, willing to give to others without complaining. Robert was There throughout the trials and tribulations in my life. When difficult times Came we fought it together. I say this to you Robert, not only are you my Husband, and you are my friend.

Lastly I dedicate this book and give love to my sisters Jerline, Linda, Gloria, and my brother Andrew. My nieces Tamika, Brittany, Nicole, TyKeara, and Ja'Brea. To my nephews Brandon, Yorel, Keon, Trey, And Gregory.

Before I end my dedication I cannot leave out four more Special people. I call them my adopted sisters, Jetta (Poochie), and Shalanda (Terri). To my aunt Ada, and second mother Myrtle. To my two God children Tye and Tyeasha. Again all of you hold a special place in my Heart. There are so many people that I would like to name, but I say this to My immediate and distant family, I Love You all. May God continue to Bless all of my people, and may God present you with His glorious presence Without fault and great joy.

ACKNOWLEDGEMENTS

Praise and Glory to my Father from heaven I Thank You for being the Great I Am, The I Am when I needed you to Be and You were.

The Great I Am in the time of my disparity, the God who sits high and looks low and knows everyone's situation.

The God who listens, and the God who delivers I can't thank you enough from the bottom of my heart. If there is anything that I can do for you, I will myself before you.

I thank Deanna for believing in me, and helping me give back to God. You are a living testimony. I thank my mother, daughter, husband, friends, family, pastors, enemies and doctors for the role you all played in my life. Once again I Thank You God for being my Jehovah Jireh, my provider.

FOREWORD

Angel In A Tent is written by Saundra Mills. In 1996 God had given her a revelation for this assignment. She wants the readers to know that storms will come. While the storms are coming you will get through, The Power of God was directing her to do so. After her sickness, The Spirit of God was transforming her into what he wanted for her life. When Angel In a Tent was being developed she would turn everything off in the house, as she began meditating, opening up the Word of God, and started reading. She read and read, searching and searching as if she was looking for the finest piece of jewelry; her flesh said put that Bible down, but her spirit said no!!!! Search, go, and read on, she continue to read. The pen is in her hand and she started writing, she began writing down her feeling about what she was going through.

One day she was at this copying center and she met this lady named Deanna. As she was printing the pages from her writing, Deanna introduced herself and said she could help her.

So they got together and they had so much in common. They experienced almost some of the same trials. They both knew that God hands were in this, as they began to share their story. They both know who God is. Deanna and Saundra continue to talk. As Angel in a Tent was being born she had to get everything out of her. It was like a woman in labor. It had to be released; she could no longer consume carrying it anymore. Then Angel In A Tent was born. The true test of faith is standing strong during adversity.

This book has been a blessing to me and I pray that it will help guide you to that peaceful place that is within and give you the tools you need to walk in victory.

Makele Harrison

PREFACE

Angel In A Tent will enlighten the readers minds. It will bring a sense of awareness in how a person might examine themselves. After reading Angel In A Tent it should bring belief, faith, and deliverance, encouragement, awareness, repentance, healing, confession, and allow people to think, see, and know that God owns the universe. You will know that in all things God hand is at work in everything. The storms and trials will come, but know that you are not in this alone. God is there to protect us.

For those of us who call ourselves believers in Christ. We must do our job to expose the enemy. The enemy's job is to keep us in darkness and never tell. The devil is a liar. I say shout it from the roof top!!!! Take back your power. "Believers claim your victory through the Anointed One!"

So I share Angel In A tent with the world young and old. Have an open heart and mind. Stop placing God in a box. Allow yourself to vision God in all things. For he is worthy of the praise.

Contents

Dedication   vii
Acknowledgements   ix
Foreword   xi
Preface   xiii
Introduction   xix

Chapter 1 — O, Magnify Yahweh   **1**
Sustenance   3
Meat   5
Bread Of Life   7
Water   9
Mercy   11
Three   13
Thank You   15
What's His Name?   19
How Do I Spell Relief?   21
When I Am Walking   23
In The Image of Yahweh   25
How Sweet Is Love…How Sweet It Is   27
Knowing When To Step In.   29

Chapter 2 — Brighter Hope   **31**
Struggling With The Flesh   33
Light At the End of the Tunnel   35
I Saw Her   37
Brighter Hope   38
Could've Been Worse   39
Find Peace and Happiness   41
Smile   43
Beauty Within   45
I Wish   47
No Matter How It Seems   49
Hush Baby   51
Rob From A Smile   53
The Lost   **55**
Never Doubt   57
Miracles   63

Chapter 3 — Angel In A Tent   **65**
Angel In A Tent   67

Chapter 4 — A Walking Tabernacle   73

Body Language   75
The Hand   77
The Feet   79
The Mouth   85
The Back   87
The Mind   89
The Heart   93
The Ear   95

Chapter 5 — The Ties That Bind   97

Young Mother   99
You   103
He, She, They   105
The Ties That Bind   106
Admonishment in the Family   107
Generation neXt   111
Greet One Another   115
Big Kids   117
Little Children   119
Mother   123
She   125
Sisters   127
Daughter   129
The Ties That Bind   130
Big Brother   131
Son   135

Chapter 6 — The Trumpet's Growl   137

Observation of the Human Condition   139
Do You Know Where We're Going?   143
The Peacemaker   147
Never Entertain The Devil   151
Closing The Door   153
Never Before   155
Confusion   159
Light or Dark   161
What the World Needs   163
Deal With It   165
Ignorance and Arrogance   171
Scars   175
Mastering What's In You   177
Contagious   182
Weakness   187

Chapter 7 — The Beginning, The End and Everything in Between   189

Images   191
Take It Away   213
Chasing After the Wind   215
A Seed Of Truth   217
We All Grieve   221
Love   225
He's Not a Genie   227
I Surrender   229
Riding In My Car   231
Heavenly   233
Touch The Hem Of His Garment   235
The Flesh   239
BLOOD   244
Piercing   249
The Cross   255
I Have Risen   257
Haven't You Heard   259
What I Like About Christmas   267
My Story   269
Death To Rebirth   273
It Could Be You   277
Patience   283
Breaking Bread   293
The King Of Glory   299
The Man   303
Dreams   307
Therapy   309
Position   315
He Will Humble   323
Secrets   327
The names of God   331

Appendix - Key Points   341

Songs To Him In The Tabernacle   345

BE STILL   347
Change   348
DREAMS   351
FAITH   352
His Faithfulness   354
I am THAT I am   355
Jehovah   356
The Voice   357

Man Up   361
MY GRACE   363
Praises   365
Return To He   366
Salt And Light   367
Amen! He's Coming Soon   368
ABBA   370
MY GRACE   372
Touched By Him   373

INTRODUCTION

Angel In A Tent is written first and for most to my Lord and Savior Yashua Jesus. The writings are from some revelation that One had experience.

Angel In A Tent are filled with short stories , that are Express through poetry , prayers , repentance , awareness , faith , and Testimonies . The vision for doing this assignment was from the True And Living GOD . When GOD stepped into my life. He was the **One** who Delivered me from the bondage that was holding me down . I dedicate This book to my first love my Lord and Savior.

My testimony is what GOD has done for me .When GOD paid a visit to me . He showed me that I was nothing but a vessel. GOD broke me into pieces . He shape , mold , and uphold me . After doing His work in me . A revelation came to me , as I saw with My own eyes of His Glory .

Now while GOD was doing His work on me . It was a Process and not a pretty picture . It was a lot of work , pulling off The layers and layers of all the stuff that was hidden in darkness . "As I shout ! Nothing is to hard for GOD . For He is The Great I Am . GOD will go after the one whom He love . I know the meaning of being Broken and married to a backslider .

You know I thought that I had it all together . I did go To church , and you could say that's what I did . I went to church Service Sunday after Sunday this is what I did . As I can only speak For myself I was empty .

In 1996 GOD touched me and I knew that I will never Be the same again . GOD left His mark on me and in me . It was a new Birth . I felt renewed and whole as a person . I began praising Him , Thanking Him for dividing His Word Of Truth . I started acknowledging Him , and sharing Him with others. In doing Angel In A Tent I prayed That it will reach as many people as He intended it to be reached for His Kingdom . I know that I can't reach the people inside the walls of The church. For that is not my assignment . But for most of the church Goers they say that they are born again and have it all together . I Thought the same thing , until I was able to see with my spiritual eyes That I was wrong. Yes we hear the psalmist sing praises and worship In the Sanctuary , but that is temporary . "Glory Hallelujah ! When one Develop a relationship ." Yes! A relationship with just you and the Almighty this is forever . No one can take that away . When GOD touched Me . I cried out for an earnest prayer of deliverance from superficial things, From myself , all the negative things that was surrounding me. I needed More of Him, less of me , and help was on the way .

My assignment for Angel In A Tent are intended for Sinners who are real , in need of help , not knowing where to turn ,and Will not be criticize of their short coming . When reading Angel In A Tent I pray that the readers will receive some comfort, compassion, and awe. This book Angel In A Tent want people to know that it's alright to go to Others for help in some situation , but there is no One like our True GOD. He is there to listen to the report , come back, and have the answers to every Problem and solution . But first we must get honest with ourselves, Surrender and give one self to the LORD. After doing that He will show His Light and you will be enlighten by Him for honoring His commandments.

I can relate to the issues that one may have, for I had Been there and I could not turn to people . The Spirit would not allow me To do so . I had to go through this alone . I had to empty myself before GOD. My GOD listened to my request , and He showed me what I had To do . First I had to repent to Him , asking Him to forgive me and come In and sit with me for I am a sinner . Please LORD come and rescue me From this body of death . I needed a relationship with GOD , and I wanted It bad . I began diligently seeking after Him . I didn't care about anything. I lost things and myself. I was my worst enemy . Now I truly understand What Paul meant by struggling with the flesh . It really was a battle ,but Thanks be to The Almighty . He didn't leave me there . GOD is a deliver And True Friend. After helping me in my time going through those dark Area of my life . GOD showed me that He demand respect , obedience, Reverence , and that it's never about self . He get the Glory . So for seeing, And what I knew. He get reverence , respect , obedience and everything . I died to the flesh , denied myself , carried my own cross and I followed Him . This was a heavy cross to hold, and everyone has their own cross .

GOD has place this assignment in my heart, and I   Have to do His will . I know that I would never get the opportunity to speak GOD Word in the church for I am not a founder of any church . For the church live in me . This assignment ,GOD told me to give it to Those who are outcast. For I have been there and walked in those Same shoes . I have learned to trust GOD and Him only .I learned to Allow Him to be Who He said that He was. I learned to trust , let go, Get out of His way, as He performed His mighty work . Do know it is Never about man-kind . It's   all about our Maker and Creator to manifest Himself in our mortal body , and when we yield to Him . GOD revelation And deliverance will come . When He said that He is The First and Last Alpha and

Omega , The Beginning and End . GOD has spoken and Truly I do reverence Him . I pray that this book Angel In A Tent will Help as many people , who are going through obstacle in their life , and Know that you are never alone . GOD is always with you even though You can't see Him . His Spirit live in us . So began to walk by faith. Start Believing , trusting , and reverencing Him. Do give every situation , circumstance, problem all to Him and He will make you free.

O, Magnify Yahweh

Psalms 34:3
*O magnify Yahweh with me, and
let us exhalt his name together*

O, Magnify Yahweh

Sustenance
ISAIAH 55:6 Turn to the LORD and pray to Him ,
Now that He is near .

HEBREW 11:1 To have faith is to be sure of the
Things we hope for , to be certain of the things we
Cannot see .

Sustenance

Can't walk without it
Can't talk without it
Can't sleep without it
Can't even breathe without it.

Builds my strength .
Harnesses my gifts
Broadens my mind
Gives me life .

It nourishes .
Maintains.
Sustains .
Supports .

If I can't walk or talk
Sleep or breath,
There is no life .

If I want strength and gifts,
A sound mind and life abundantly ,
I must have it .

I need nourishment continuously
To maintain good health
That sustains me when I'm in need .

Yashua is the Sustenance
That allows me to walk and talk
Sleep and breathe .
He builds my strength
Develops my gifts
Expands my mind
Brings me life abundantly
He nourishes and maintains

Sustains and supports
Where there is no
Sustenance
There is no life.

O, Magnify Yahweh

Meat
1PETER 1: 19, 20 It was the costly sacrifice of Christ,
Who was like a lamb without defect or flow .

He had been chosen by God before the creation of
The world and revealed in these last days for your sake .

Meat

Do you doubt
The Creator will provide ?
From the foundation of the world
He promised thing that live
Shall be meat for you;
Even as the green herb
Have I given you all things."
Even greater than the meat
To eat
For the body's desire ,
Is the meat of the Lamb in me .

God's chosen people-
Ignorant of His ultimate plan,
Were commanded to kill and eat
A perfect lamb without spot or blemish.
Pharaoh's lot near at hand
Hurriedly ,
Unknowingly,
They executed the Master's plan.
Those obedient to the command
From the death angel were saved.

Like wise, in this land of the Nile,
Armageddon on the horizon,
Jews and Gentiles alike
Commanded by the Almighty
To eat
"Then Yashua said unto them,
Verily, Verily, I saw unto you ,
Except ye eat the flesh of the Son of man,
And drink His blood ,
Ye have no life in you."
"Whoso eat my flesh,
And drink my blood ,

Hath eternal life;
And I will raise him up
At the last day ."

The Son proclaims
His flesh to be meat indeed!
Unless He is in us,
We , too shall perish.

So much greater
Than meat to eat
To fill the body's desire
Is the meat of the Lamb in me.

O, Magnify Yahweh

Bread Of Life
JOHN 6:33 For the bread of God is He who comes down from
Heaven and gives life to the world ."

Bread Of Life

When the Israelites where rescued
From Pharaoh's mighty grip
And led through the wilderness,
Manna from heaven
To satisfy their physical need
Freely given
Daily .

When the Messiah walked the Earth
Left in Capernaum a message for the ages
Likening the Exodus from Egypt
The daily bread in the wilderness
He is the true bread
The Bread of life
Come from heaven.

Come to Him
Never hunger
He is our Daily Bread .___

O, Magnify Yahweh

Water
ISAIAH 48:21 When the LORD led His people through
A hot , dry desert , they did not suffer from thirst .
He made water come from a rock for them ;
He split the rock open , and water flowed out .

JOHN 7:38 As the scripture says , whoever believes in
Me , streams of life-giving water will pour out from
His heart .

Water

Oh, the gentle nurturing of water
Descends from the clouds
Kissing the earth's soil
Bringing forth fruit
To eat .

Oh, the magnificent beauty of water
Descends from the heavens
Forms streams and lakes
Oceans and seas
Supporting life in the waters
Majestic springs
Pure, blue waves
Soothing blanket shore-side.

Oh, the mighty power of water
Massive tidal waves
Torrential rains
Monsoon
Devastating floods
Suffocating humidity
Slow, murdering droughts

Oh, the living water
That nurtures life like a mother to her child
Is magnificent in beauty like the Niagara
Is powerful and mighty
Bringing Earth to her knees
Taking away what He only can give.

Oh, the nurturing
Beautiful
Powerful Living Water.

How gracious is the Creator
To rain on the just

And the unjust.
Without water
There is no life.

O, Magnify Yahweh

Mercy
ROMANS 11:32 For God has made all people prisoners
Of disobedience , so that He might show mercy to them all.

Mercy

Mercy , mercy , mercy on me
This is my fervent plea;
That Your grace forever be
 Sufficient even for me.

Daily I fight the enemy
That rages in me
A duel to the death
A battle I lose daily.

When will pride subside?
A lamp to my feet are Your words.
Still I fumble in the dark
Even with the knowledge
Plainly seen:
Pride comes before the fall .

A true follower of Your will
I sincerely want to be
Yet Paul to the Roman I echo,
"For the good that I will to do,
I do not do;
But the evil I will not do,
That I practice."

I dishonor my brother
Scorn my sister
With harsh words and
Two- faced deeds.
Yet no mercy I show
When the same falls on me.

My true El
Surely You are.
Your mercy great,
Your anger slow.

Still I know
You will not always withhold
Your wrath.

Mercy, mercy, mercy on me
This is my fervent plea;
That Your grace forever be
Sufficient even for me.

O, Magnify Yahweh

Three
PSALMS 37:4 Seek your happiness in the LORD
And He will give you your heart's desire .

Three

I asked the Lord
To give me three a day .

And when I prayed,
This is what I heard
The Lord say,

When you pray ,
Know that it is three
Working together .
Ask in my name
And I will give thee.

So I prayed this prayer:
Lord give me three a day .
The vision
The inspiration
The direction.

I did this every day
And He deserves
The praise.

He helped me to
Realize my vision
Propelled by His inspiration
And pointed me in the right direction.

He withheld nothing good from me.
He gave me all three .

O, Magnify Yahweh

Thank you
EPHESIANS 3:20 To Him who by means of His power
Working in us is able to do so much more than we can
Ever ask for, or think of.

Thank You

Thank you, Yashua
For your love toward me.
Love that is incomprehensible.
That you would lay down your life me.

Thank you, Yashua
For your limitless grace.
That gives me yet one more chance.
To reach that heavenly place.

Thank you, Yashua
For your purpose, pattern, and plan.
Your marvelous handiwork.
That you've been plane to man.

What manner of love is this
That offers me an eternity of peace.
From pain, darkness and destruction.
Thank you, Yashua
For the hope of this sweet relief.

O, Magnify Yahweh

Patiently
JAMES 5:8 You also must be patient. Keep your hopes
High, for the day of the Lord's coming is near .

O, Magnify Yahweh

Patiently
JAMES 5:8 You also must be patient. Keep your hopes
High, for the day of the Lord's coming is near .

O, Magnify Yahweh

What's His Name
EXODUS 34:5,6 The LORD came down in a cloud, stood
With him there, and pronounce His holy name, The LORD.

And He passed in front of Moses proclaiming "The LORD
The LORD, the compassionate and gracious God, slow to
Anger, abounding in love and faithfulness.

JOHN 1:1 In the beginning was the Word, and the Word
Was with God, and the Word was God.

REVELATION 22:13 I Am the Alpha and the Omega, the
First and the Last, the Beginning and the End.

What's His Name?

What's His name?
Yashua is His name.
It's the name
That you can stand on
When you're in trouble.
Yashua is His name.

What's His name?
Yashua is His name.
It's the kind of name
You can call on
When you need a friend.
Yashua is His name.

What's His name?
It's the name to call
In the late night hour.
Yashua is His name.

What's His name?
Yashua is His name.
It's the name you call on
When you see no way out.
Yashua is His name.

What's His name?
His name is Yashua
Yashua is His name.

O, Magnify Yahweh

How Do I Spell Relief
HEBREW 2:16-18 For it is clear that it is not the angels
That He helps. Instead, as the scripture says "He helps
The descendants of Abraham."

This , means that He had to become like His brothers in
Every way, in order to be their faithful and merciful High
Priest in His service to God, so that the people's sins would
Be forgiven.

And now He can help those who are tempted, because He
Himself was tempted and suffered.

How Do I Spell Relief?

How Do I Spell Relief?

Like this:

Y-   Yesterday the same as today.
A-   Abiding within me.
S-   Separating me to His salvation
H-   Humbling me
U-   Understanding daily He gives me.
A-   Always the King of Glory.
When I put my relief all together.
I thank Y A S H U A for a
Yearning to
Always,
Search for the truth and for
Understanding of that truth which
Always gives salvation.
What a relief!

O, Magnify Yahweh

When I Am Walking
ROMANS 11:36 For all things were created by Him,
And for Him. To God be the glory forever! Amen.

When I Am Walking

When I am walking
What do I see?
I see birds and the trees.

When I am walking
What do I see?
I see the Creator
The sky's moon and Sun.

When I am walking
What do I see?
I see the Creator
The grass and the flowers.

When I am walking
What do I see?
I see the Creator
People walking like you and me.
It's the Savior I really see.

He walks with me
And talks with me
I hear His song in the wind
I feel His tears in the rain
I imagine His joy in the Sun
I know His grace at dusk
Promising a new day
Another chance
To walk and see
The Creator-The Savior
That lives everywhere
Even in me.

O, Magnify Yahweh

In The Image Of Yahweh
Exodus 25:8-40 And let them make me a sanctuary; that I may
Dwell among them.

Exodus 25:9 According to all that I show thee after the pattern
Of the tabernacle, and the pattern of all the instruments thereof,
Ever so shall ye make it.

Exodus 25:10........And they shall make an ark of shittim wood:
Two cubits and half shall be the length thereof, and a cubit and
A half the height thereof.

Exodus 25:19...........And make the cherub on the one end, and
The other cherub on the other end: even of the mercy seat shall
Ye make the cherubim on the two ends thereof.

Exodus 25:31........And thou shall make the candlestick of pure
Gold; of beaten work shall the candlestick be made, his shaft, and
His branches, his bowls, his knops, and flowers, shall be of the
Same.

Exodus 25:40 And look that thou make them after their pattern,
Which was showed thee in the mount.

In The Image of Yahweh

How excellent is His creation.
All that is made
Is made in His likeness.
Without Him was nothing made
That was made.

To understand His image
Spy the book of Exodus
On the mount,
The pattern given.
For the first time
Man can understand.

What it means
To be made in His image
It's not just looks
But an entire plan in question.
Following the pattern
Which is Yahweh Elohim
The Original Pattern.

How excellent is His creation
All that is made
Is made in His likeness.
And after His own pattern.
Without Him was nothing made
That was made.

O, Magnify Yahweh

How Sweet Is Love…How Sweet It Is
COLOSSIANS 3:14 And to all these qualities add love,
Which binds all things together in perfect unity.

How Sweet Is Love…How Sweet It Is

Sweet, sweet, sweet, is love.
Love is sweet, love is kind.
Love is always on my mind.

Sweet, sweet, sweet is love
Like a warm, tight hug
From a remorseful little toddler.
Sweet, sweet, sweet is love.

Like the prodigal Son.
Back from the grave
Father unmoved by his going astray.
How sweet is love.

A mother weeps in joy
At the sight of her boy
Becoming a man
Leaving for the land.
Of learning.
How sweet is love.

The Sun shining through.
After days of flooding rains
God's Grace,
How sweet is love.

Pouring rain comes
Drowning out the suffocating drought
Oh, how sweet is love.

It's that love
That brings peace
It's that love
That brings joy
It's that Love
That brings understanding

Oh, How sweet is Love

Sweet, sweet, sweet is love
Love is sweet, love is kind.
Love is always on my mind.

27

O, Magnify Yahweh

Knowing When To Step In
PSALMS 136 :3-4 Give thanks to the mightiest of all
Lord's His love is eternal.

He alone performs great miracles, His love is eternal.

Knowing When To Step In.

Like a broken clay pot
I was in pieces.
Then You stepped in.

Like a deer
Frozen by oncoming lights,
I was paralyzed
And couldn't cross over to the other side.

When I thought I knew
And didn't know
That I didn't know
I didn't know
Then You stepped in.

When I get tired
Of doing it my way
And was ready for a new roadway.
Then You stepped in.

You know just when
To step right on in.
You are the potter that mended the pieces
And the driver who helped me cross over
To the other side of the road.

You are the patient teacher
Who instructs me so that I can understand.
You are the construction engineer
With the blueprints for my life.

Your anointing power fell upon me.
Your precious Holy Spirit made me free.

I am born again.
I am whole again.

You are my deliverer and
My Redeemer.

And I say thank Yashua.
I will always praise your
Name.
And I give You all the honor
And glory.

And I do truly thank you,
Yashua for knowing when
When to step in.

Brighter Hope

Psalms 31:24:

Be of good courage, and He shall
Strengthen your heart, all ye that
Hope in Yahweh Elohim.

Brighter Hope

Struggling With The Flesh
ROMANS 8:11 If the Spirit of God, who raised Jesus from death
Lives in you, then He who raised Christ from death will also give life
To your mortal bodies by the presence of His Spirit in you.

Struggling With The Flesh

The Apostle Paul
Says it best.
"For what I would,
That do I not;
But what I hate,
That do I."

An everyday occurrence
Is this battle with the flesh.
Unclean deeds
Unclean thoughts
You can't escape it.

But, wait…
There is always a ram in the bush.

Paul lamented
That he be rescued
From his flesh.
And so he was.
Healed from his sickness.
With Yashua in him.
No more to be condemned.

There is therefore now
No condemnation
To them which are in Yashua the
Messiah,
Who walk not after the flesh,
But after the Spirit.

We will never reach a place
Where we are so holy
And sanctified
And set apart
That we will not be tested.

Indeed the time has come
When the test is on
And if you are not Yashua
Surely you will fail.

While He is still near
Call on the name of Yashua
A contrite spirit
A humble heart
These He will pardon abundantly.

For to be carnally minded is death;
But to be spiritually minded
Is life and peace.

Don't struggle.
You can't win.
The only One who can
Is Yashua the Messiah.
He is the ram in the bush.
He is the escape plan.
He is the Holy Spirit
He is life and peace.

Brighter Hope

Light At The End of The Tunnel

ISAIAH 65:1 The LORD said, " I was ready to answer
My people's prayer, but they did not pray. I was ready
For them to find me, but they did not even try. The nation
Did not pray to me, even though I was always ready to
Answer, "Here I Am; I will help you.

Light At the End of the Tunnel

There is a light at the end
Of the tunnel.

What tunnel?
The tunnel of darkness
Typifying ignorance.

This light
At the end of the tunnel:
It's bright
And shines like
No ordinary light.
It has no on and off switch.

You cry, and groan
The tunnel is long.
You search and moan.
The tunnel is dark.

Why would you want
To live your life in the dark
Knowing full well you can't see.

This light
I tell you,
At the end of the tunnel:
It's bright
And shines like
No ordinary light.
You will know
That by it you are illuminated
When no longer you
Search and moan
Cry and groan.
And by the way,
This light is eternal.

Brighter Hope

I Saw Her
REVELATION 22:12 " Listen! Says Jesus. "I Am coming soon!
I will bring my rewards with me, to give to each one according to
What he has done.

REVELATION 22:20 He who gives his testimony to all this says,
"Yes indeed! I Am coming soon! "So be it. Come, Lord Jesus!

I Saw Her

I saw her sitting where the brethren gather.
She sits with dignity.
Always ready to give a helping hand.

When the children speak out loud
She seems to know how to calm them down.

I see her all the time.
We sometimes exchange kind but brief greetings.
But I never get to know her.

I see her come to the building
Sunday after Sunday.

But this Sunday
Something was difference about her.

I could see her brokenness.
I could feel her pain.

When the choir began to sing
She would weep and weep.
I saw her.
I said this to her.
You are seeking Yahweh
While He may yet be found.
This is a process we all go through.
Always know in the process
Yahweh is testing you.
He loves you.
Why else would He lead you here?
He's courting you
Wants to marry you
So, do tarry here.
My sister, be of good cheer.
The Bridegroom is Coming!

Brighter Hope

Could've Been Worse
2CORINTHIANS 4:16-18 For this reason we never become discouraged.
Even though our physical being is gradually decaying, yet our spiritual
Being is renewed day after day.

And this small and temporary trouble we suffer will bring us a tremendous
And eternal glory, much greater than the trouble.

For we fix our attention, not on things that are seen, but on things that are
Unseen . What can be seen lasts only for a time, but what cannot be seen Lasts
forever.

Could've Been Worse

I was sick in bed with a flu.
Coughing, body in all sorts of pain.
I started t complain.

"I'm sick and I'm tired.
Coughing hurts, my throat is soar.
My body aches
Wiping sneezes are worse."

By His grace
I came to my senses.
With all my aches and pains
I have eternal life.
This discomfort is temporal.
Just for a minute
In Yahweh's sight.
I will soon have a glorified body
Without sickness or pain.
Praising my Savior forevermore.

Now when I think on this
The Pain subsides.
He could've left me in the world
Ignorant of my state and fate.
Now that could've been worse.

Brighter Hope

Find Peace and Happiness
PROVERBS 18:10 The LORD is like a strong tower, where the
Righteous can go and be safe.

Find Peace and Happiness

How can I find peace and happiness?
Peace and happiness are found within.
A willing heart is all that is required.

Be still for a moment
Mind set on the Messiah.
Hear the sounds around you
Purposefully.
Breathe deeply, slowly
Rest in Him.

Here Him say,
"Finally, brethren, whatsoever things are true,
Whatsoever things are honest,
Whatsoever things are just,
Whatsoever things are pure,
Whatsoever things are lovely,
Whatsoever things are of good report;
If there be any virtue,
And if there be any praise,
Think on these things."

The thoughts within
Determine the acts without
Think on the things that He commands
Therein lies peace and happiness.

Brighter Hope

Smile
PROVERBS 15:30 Smiling faces make you happy, and good news
Makes you feel better.

Smile

Smile
Everyday.
It'll change your state of mind
In every way.

Smile
It doesn't hurt.
Takes less than a frown
It's really not hard work.

Smile
Even when the enemy is on the attack.
His darts become Nerf turf .
He'll probably turn back.

Smile
While it's still day.
The enemy will return at night.
Greet him with a smile
He'll again take flight.

Smile
When there's something to smile about
And even when there's not.
What do you have to lose?
Nothing. A smile doesn't charge a lot.

Smile
Everyday.
It'll change your state of mind
In every way._

Brighter Hope

Beauty Within
1CORINTHIANS 2:10 But it was to us that God made known His
Secret by means of His Spirit. The Spirit searches everything, even
The hidden depths of God's purpose.

1CORINTHIANS 3:16 Surely you know that you are God's temple
and that God's Spirit lives in you!

Beauty Within

One day I was looking into the mirror
I was getting all dolled up.

I was about to apply the mask
When I suddenly stopped

I looked to my left
There was my eye shadow.

I looked in the middle
There was my lipstick .

I looked to my right.
There was my face powder.

The tools were in place
I was ready for the mask.

I looked into the mirror again.
This time I heard the spirit say,
Beauty comes from within.

Forget about the masks
That you masquerade in
And look again.
Beauty comes from within.

Love who you are.
Be pleased with yourself.
Become your best friend.

Makeup can't cover
The spirit within
Be it negative or positive,
The spirit cannot be hidden.

Carefully apply His words
To your heart.
And His will to your life.
Then you can see
The inner beauty that is
Within.

Brighter Hope

I Wish
COLOSSIANS 3:2 Keep your minds fixed on things above, not on
Things here on earth.

MATHEW 7:7-8 "Ask, and you will receive; seek, and you will find;
Knock and the door will be opened to you.

For everyone who asks will receive, and anyone who seek will find,
And the door will be opened to him who knocks.

I Wish

I wish I could be like my neighbors.
I wish I were a movie star.
I wish I had lots of money.
I wish I had a brand new Lexus.
I wish I had a lot of friends.
I wish I had a big, beautiful house
With a white picket fence.
I wish I had a tall, handsome and kind husband.
I wish I had a child.
I wish my children were grown.
I wish I'd never have to work again.

With all those wishes that you may have,
Have you stopped to think that
God plays a role in everything?

If you keep God first
And foremost in your life,
Seek the kingdom and it's righteousness,
He will give you the desire of your heart.

So stop wishing that you had
What your eyes think is good.
Physical treasures are no match
For spiritual ones.

Pray to the Lord
Ask for eternal riches.
Turn your "I wish " to
"Father, Your will be done."
Open up the windows of heaven
And pour upon you gifts
Too numerous to count.

Your desires He will fulfill.
If you but say ,"Father Your will."

Brighter Hope

No Matter How It Seems
REVELATION 1:8 "I Am the First and the Last, "says the Lord God Almighty, Who is, Who was, and Who is to come.

No Matter How It Seems

No matter how it seems,
It's not how it looks
There's a message behind
The picture
No matter how it seems._

Brighter Hope

Hush Baby
DEUTERONOMY 7:9 Remember that the LORD your God is the only God and that He is faithful. He will keep His covenant and show His Constant love to a thousand generations of those who love Him and obey His commands.

Hush Baby

Hush, baby don't say a word.
I know your secret.
I won't tell the birds.

Hush, baby your secret is safe with me.
I have my finger on you.
Hush, baby don't say a word.

Satan whispered so sweet and gentle.
I looked out the window in pain
At birds perched
On the evergreen trees below.

I will tell the mocking birds
So he said.
Well, devil, do as you please.
I have carried this pain
Forever it seems.
I do have an El that loves me.
His Spirit spoke in my soul.

I Am Yahweh.
I Am your Elohim.
Let it all go.
I Am greater than he.
He can't touch your soul.
I've chosen you.
He attacked your body.
Thinking He's got control.
It was necessary to humble you this way.
To make room for my occupancy.

It's my Spirit that saved you.
My Spirit led you through.

I have given you a revelation.
The devil is a liar.
I Am Yahweh.

Remember the words I spoke to you.
Those who are last will be first.
Blessed are the meek.
Blessed are the peace makers.
For they will be called the sons of Yahweh.

I Am the Alpha and the Omega.
The First and the Last.
The Beginning and the End.

I Am Yahweh
So don't hush, baby
Do say a word
I Am your Elohim
Who controls the birds.

Brighter Hope

Rob From A Smile

PSALMS 107:19 Then they cried out to the LORD in their trouble,
And He saved them from their distress.

Rob From A Smile

Feeling sad and disappointed,
A smile went away from me today.
The happiness, joy, and peace were
gone.

It led me to do an about face.
And to think things over in another
way.
When doing this,
All the energy and strength was taken
from me.
It almost took charge over me.

I had to be still, and listen from within.
Father so I said, I can't do this alone.
I need for You to help me with this.
As I waited for my Father's will.

His Spirit spoke to my spirit,
My child He said, you can be at rest,
Give it all to Me, for I know what's
best.

His power from within, help me to
realize,
That my smile will be brought back to
me again.
His Spirit spoke, listen to Me, and
stop
Burning yourself out from all that
negativity.

He encouraged me that you are free.
"Go!
You are free, spread your wings and fly
Like an Eagle. **"Go!**

Take charge and control of yourself
from
Outward and in. **"Do!**
You are the one who's able to go
through. **"Do!**
It's all inside of you, encouraging me
to come,
Walk through. **"Go!**
Do what I Am telling you, and never
allow
That wasted energy to rob you again.
"Do!
It's a dual to the battle, but you will
win. **"Do!**
That smile can never be taken from you
again,
For My Spirit live within, and I Am
the **One**,
That can help you over and over again.
That smile, or what- ever it may be,
I Am the One who holds, and sees the
outcome
For your destiny.
As long as you realize, that **I Live, I
Live, I Live.**
And **My** encouragement lies from
within.

It's **My Spirit** that touched your spirit.
And **I will** replace what happens inside
of you again.
That willingness of **My Smile, My Joy,
My Peace,**
And **I will** be the **One**, to renew
everything **I** see
That is fit for your life.
So smile for your beauty lies from
within.

Brighter Hope

The Lost
ECCLESIASTES 3:1 There is a time for everything,
And a season for every activity under heaven.

The Lost

Stirring at the photographs . it took me
back in reminiscing.
The times when we were children at
play.
Then I put the strap book back in it 's
rightful place.
Retiring myself for the night.
The next day drama came this way.
Tribulation walked into my life.
It took control over me, and not
knowing when it was
Going to end.
It lead me in another direction.
"Asking question, after question?
How could this be? Lord come and
take control over me.
Was I the one who cause this to be?
Please, Lord come and search me.

You are the Only One who knows my
heart.
Bring me back to the understanding ,
And to that person , who I use to be.
Come Lord please do search me.
My Lord make me free.
Remove all those barriers out of my
way.
Come Lord, while I am kneeling to
pray.

I'm praying to you earnestly.
And asking the will of my Father.
Help me through the disappointments,
the pains,
The shadows, the valleys , and storms.

Oh please Lord talk to me.
Could You bring back to me the will of
my dreams?
Could You give back to me the
control, and self esteem,
That was taken from my life?
Could You place everything back into
my hands?
That You see fit, and what's best for
me.
My Precious Lord do restore me.

Come Lord, rescue me.
Rescue me , and make me free.
Come Lord, rescue me.
Rescue me , and make me free.
This is my earnest prayer to you Abba.

Brighter Hope

Never Doubt
PSALMS 16:10 The King speaks with divine authority;
His decisions are always right.

Never Doubt

There maybe times in your life
When you're unsure of what to do.
It may be a wayward child
Or a major shift in a relationship.
You may be unclear about finances,
Or forgoing ahead with a new job.

Never doubt for one moment
That Yahweh doesn't know your circumstance
There is a multiplicity of forks in the road
And the Master has the map for them all.
Indeed, He numbers the hairs on your head
And put together this very complex form
We call the physical body.

Be still, get quiet.
Go to your favorite room in your house.
Your secret hiding place.
Meet your Maker there.
Get comfortable.
Do away with form and fashion.
Get real and get honest.
Your Maker is not above the clouds.
He is and always has been right here with you.

Now when you understand
That He is everything and everywhere,
Close your eyes
There in your comfortable room
In your comfortable space,
And simply
Be.

Just do the thing
That He alone directs:
Breath

Breathe
Breathe
Breathe

Listen quietly now
Consciously seek to hear
That still small voice within.

You may hear
Your voice
Distracting your concentration
Saying things like:
'This is stupid.'
'This doesn't work.
It never had and never will.'
'This is a waste of time.'

Difficult it may be at first
To quiet that doubting voice.
But if you want peace
And clarity of direction
Just stay there
And be.
For we wrestle not with flesh and blood
But with principalities and powers…

You must continue
To be still
Until
Your voice quiets
And the Spirit begins
To speak peace.

You must continue
To be still
And breathe
Until
You hear whispers

Of Authority.

Listen
You've got to put in some time
Don't expect the blessing to come
In five minutes.
Your days are full of activity and noise.
It takes time to peel away
The noise, stress, and negativity.

Hear the Spirit gently say,
I am the Way, The Truth, and the Life.
Do you call Him a liar?
If He is everything and everywhere
Your circumstance is not out of His reach.
He is your circumstance.
Everything that happens
Every circumstance or situation
Just is.

This is His movie.
He's the director
And we all are actors in it.
If you know the role you want to play
The hero or the villain
You will know what you need to do.

In this human experience,
Doubt is an annoying neighbor
Always coming to visit
At the most inconvenient time.
But you can ignore his presence
Be cold and uninviting.
Go to your secret hiding place.
Meet your Maker there.
Tarry for a while
Tarry often
And simply

Be Still
Breathe
Listen
For the Voice
Of Authority

Brighter Hope

Miracles
PSALM 86:10 You are mighty and do wonderful
Things you alone are God.

Miracles

Miracles do happen.
It's a miracle you and I can see.
Anything about our Creator
Because of our staunch vanity.

It's a miracle that Yashua
From the foundation of the world
Chose you or I to see
How great is His mercy
To you and me.
What a miracle!

2Corinthians 4:17
Now the **Lord** is the **Spirit**,
And where the **Spirit** of the **Lord** is,
There is **freedom**.

Angel In A Tent

Exodus 33:10

And all the people saw the cloudy
Pillar stand at the tabernacle door:
And all the people rose up and
Worshipped, every man in his **tent**
Door.

Angel In A Tent

HEBREW 2:1 That is why we must hold on all the more
Firmly to the truths we have heard, so that we will not be
Carried away.

ISAIAH 44:24-26 I Am the LORD, Your Savior; I AM
The One who created you. I Am the LORD, the Creator
Of all things. I alone stretched out the heavens. When I
Made the earth, no one helped Me.

I make fools of fortune tellers and frustrate the predictions
Of astrologers. The words of the wise I refute and show that
Their wisdom is foolishness.

But when My servant makes a prediction, when I send a
Messenger to reveal my plans, I make those plans and predictions
Come true. I tell Jerusalem that people will live there again, and the
Cities of Judah that they will be rebuilt. Those cities will rise from
The ruins.

Angel In A Tent

Angel in a tent
Made of epidermis
Camping out
Beneath the stars
In the wilderness

The Light in the distance `
Beckons me
Urges me
To see
Beyond the unreality
Hidden from the multitude;
To travel
The road less traveled.

At first sight of the Light
Came awareness of the Darkness
The Light clears the way.
Gently pulling me from Dark's grip.

Cradled in the warm glow
Nestled in peace
Soft assurances
Kiss my ear.
Love entangles my heart.

Safety certain, I open my eyes.
Looking back at me
From my place in the Light is
The wilderness.

Wilderness filled with tents.
Of epidermis
Camping out.

Suddenly sadness intrudes
As reality unfolds
The Light's first gift of sight.

Streets filled with children
With their babies on their tiny hips.
No regard for the human life
Brought forth.
No idea what hardships lie ahead.
No vision for their futures.
Just a status symbol that claim I'm
woman.

But they're not, they are children
with babies.
In the wilderness.

Protected by the Light
Vision now crystal.
In the wilderness
I see

A brother shoot another
Nine times.
His reward:
A label- - lord
Over a seemingly incorruptible
Empire.
He slays so many
Saving none
From the white dust;
The evil spirit that
Seems so euphoric
But sharply deceitful.

Because, after while…

I see familiar faces and places.
Sink into the cold chilly water
Clutching the life preserver
Only to once again
Look to the lord as savior.

He's certain he's lord, but he's not.
Just a child
In the wilderness.

Turning slightly in the Light
From my peripheral vision
I see

Men brutalizing women
Making themselves bigger men seem.
Slaves to the anger, lust, hate of their hearts;
Unaware of the scars left
That are long, hard to heal.
Don't even care.

Physical anatomy of a man they have
But they are not men, just children
In the wilderness.

I look
I see

Fathers and mothers, once armed
With the mighty hand of discipline
Now handcuffed by legislature,
Giving birth to an entire culture of chaos.
Lawmakers smirk
At their intended handiwork.

But it's not their handiwork.
They think they are the lawgivers
But they're not, they too, are children

The children come down and

In the wilderness.

Arranging myself
In the lap of the Light
I take in a panoramic view

Imbalance, injustice, contemptible deceit.

Dilapidated neighborhoods:
Dark skin.
Tree-lined streets,
Single-family homes:
Blue eyes.

Foreign policy
Generous aid—quick and forthcoming
…non African nations only.

Imbalance…

Jails overcrowded
Disproportionately black males
College full
Disproportionately white females.

Injustice…

A long line formed
Palms outstretched
"The Give me Syndrome"
Contagious
Spreads through generations

Quick, like a brush fire.
No self-reliance
No responsibility on the mind.

Just give me.

Everyone searching
Really searching
For fame, for fortune
For wealth, for long life.
For the thing that fills the abyss.

"Go to church!"
The preacher implores
There in those walls
From the same lips
Spills tall tales
And half truths
That gain a profit
Not a soul.
But the Book says,
"If any man shall take away form the words of
The Book of this prophecy, God shall take away
His part out of the Book of life,
And out of the holy city,
And from the things which are written
 In this Book."

Woe unto the preacher reverend
Who doesn't go by the Book.

Contemptible deceit.

From Dark's deadly grip.
Many hear
Few are chosen
To travel
The road less traveled.

This is the message
From the messengers

To the messengers:

The less traveled road
Lit by four towering road sign,

Patience.
The journey is the destination
There is never a sign reading
Dead End.

Acceptance.
God created everything.
Good and Evil
There is nothing made
That was not made
By Him.
He owns the schematics.

Tolerance.
For all things made
That were made
By Him.
Imbalance.
Injustice.
Contemptible deceit.
The ram in the bush.
Humility.
That admits
I need help,
A Savior
The Light.

I am
An angel in a tent
Of epidermis.

The Light's final gifts,

Watching
Waiting
For the
Angel in a tent.

So I can see
The other angels
That will hear
My message
From the Light
His ultimate gift
To all angels
In a tent of epidermis
Camping out
Beneath the stars

A Walking Tabernacle

Hebrews 9:11:

But the Messiah being come an high
Priest of good things to come, by a
Greater and more perfect **tabernacle**,
Not made with hands, that is to say,
Not of this building;

A Walking Tabernacle

Body Language
2CORINTHIANS 5:10 For all of us must appear before Christ to be
Judged by Him. Each one will receive what he deserves, according
To everything he has done, good or bad, in his bodily life.

Body Language

I can tell
Mmm, hmm
No.
You didn't say anything.
It was your body language.

Don't look at me that way.
Your telling on yourself.
No need to act surprised.
Body says more than you do.

Your fidgety fingers
Go ratter tat
On the wooden table
All night.

But you sat up nice and straight
When Mr. Take Another Look
Walked your way
Then clenched your jaw and fists
When he stopped to greet another sister.

You didn't have to be so curt
With Miss Snoopy Nose the other day.
I said you didn't say anything
The way you glared at her
Gave it all away.

Didn't say anything to the minister Sunday
When he stepped on your toes.
Oh, I know he didn't with his feet
But his eyes was popping
A lot in your direction.
Your face turned red.
And when you slid slight down
Right there in your seat.

I said to myself," Whoop there it is!"

No matter what you do
Your body talk doesn't lie on you.
Clean up your language.
Your body language, that is.

A Walking Tabernacle

The Hand
EXODUS 13:9 This observance will be a reminder, like something
Tied on your hand or on your forehead; it will remind you to continue
To recite and study the Law of the **LORD**, because the **LORD** brought
You out of Egypt by His great power.

The Hand

The Hand creates.
The Hand holds.
The Hand grips.
The Hand gives.
Abundantly.

The Hand is swift.
The Hand is just.
The Hand draws unto itself

Whomever is chosen.
The Hand heals.
The Hand gives
Abundantly.

The Hand is precious.
The Hand is sweet.
The Hand picks you up.
The Hand restrains you.
The Hand saves.
The Hand gives
Abundantly.

A Walking Tabernacle

The Feet
PROVEBS 4:26 Plan carefully what you do, and whatever you do
Will turn out right.

The Feet

If I take one step
He promised to take two.
My feet will move
But He'll be the One
To carry me through.

Stumble and fall
Surely I will
But He'll pick me up
Dust me off
And love me greater still.

Order my steps,
Faithful Father
Only with You
Will my feet take me farther.

Your words will light the way
And guide my feet.
To trust in you
Yes, 'tis so sweet.

Hallelujah, praise Yahweh!
For the feet
That supports the body's weight.
And if I falter
While I journey
Lead me, Father
I pray.

A Walking Tabernacle

Oh My Brown Eyes
PROVERBS 16:16 It is better much better to have
Wisdom and knowledge than gold and silver.

Oh, My Brown Eyes

There was a certain young lady
Thought herself to be prim and proper
From the good life
Nothing could stop her.

Beautiful brown eyes
From her grandmother
She did inherit.

But shamelessly she batted them
And to dear grandmother
She gave no merit.

Every night
As the clock struck ten
Her majesty, the baby
Sang her litany:

Oh, my brown eyes
So beautiful to behold.
They'll bring me fame and fortune
And riches untold.

Oh, my brown eyes
See all the things I want
That fur coat
That grand car
That towering sailboat.

Oh, my brown eyes
I see success on the horizon
Made of fancy titles
And a big corner office
And whenever I want,

Oh, my brown eyes
So beautiful to behold.
Yes, they'll bring me fame and
fortune and riches untold.

At the sound of this nagging
Lullaby.
Grandmother did frown.
But, she thought, a child, a phase
This too shall pass.
Reality will bring her down.

A woman of great patience
Usually is she
But after 99 nights of this song,
She moaned,
"How much longer will this
phase be?"

Slowly she rose
From her rocking chair
Just as the clock struck ten.

She shot up the stairs
Burst through the door
And yelled to the child,
"Sing that song, no more!"

She looked into those eyes
That were much like hers,
Place her hands on her hips
And sternly spoke these very
words:

Foolish child!
Don't even know
It's a blessing to have

A long, peaceful hiatus.
There are some out
Wish they could
Gaze flighty like you do
In the night.

All night
Every night
I hear you sing,
Grandmother said mockingly,

"Oh my beautiful brown eyes.
So beautiful to behold."
But what good are those eyes
Full of covetous pride
That only see silver and gold?

Spiritual sight
And beauty within
Are what you should covert most

God's got a championship title
A great, big mansion
And a much larger sailboat.

Life, health and strength
A serene, humble spirit
Surely these are heavenly treasures.

These diamond and sapphire blessings
Once given by Him
Are gift beyond human measure.

Yes, child these stars do shine bright
But they are not specially made for you.
He created the heavens and the earth
And He saw that it was good.

Physical sight.
Is the beauty inside you.

Before you go searching
For riches untold,
Take it from these
Beautiful brown eyes
All that glitters
Ain't gold.

Your brown eyes are beautiful
This is true
But what really matters most

A Walking Tabernacle

The Mouth
ISAIAH 55:11 So also will be the word I speak.
It will not fail to do what I plan for it; it will do
Everything I send it to do .

PROVERBS 18:20 You will have to live with the
Consequences of everything you say.

The Mouth

Use the mouth
  To speak.

Use the mouth
  To eat.

Use the mouth
  To rejoice.

Use the mouth
  To pray.

Use the mouth
  To give praises.

Use the mouth
  To give thanks.

Use the mouth
  To bless someone.

Use the mouth
  To lovingly correct.

Use the mouth
  For words of truth.

Use your mouth
  For the right things and
Yahweh will bless you.

A Walking Tabernacle

The Back
PSALMS 3:4 I call to the LORD for help, and from
His sacred hill He answers me.

The Back

Built to support the body's frame
Holding the body's message center.
Breaks a fall.
Gives way to a good night's sleep.

So many important tasks
Are the back's responsibility.
If yours is in good working order,
Sing hallelujah and praise Yahweh.

So many others have back pain
And chronic back trouble
They walk bent over
Or not at all.

If yours is in good working order,
Sing hallelujah and praise Yahweh.

If you are one of those
Who suffer with back trouble
Take heart.
Trouble don't last always.

Sometimes trouble comes to make us stronger.
Even back trouble.

When you lay outstretched on your back
Your eyes look toward heaven
And the Father watches you.

Your cries for mercy are heard
And healing will come.
Remember His word,
"For we know that if our earthly house
Of this tabernacle were dissolved,
We have a building of Yahweh,
An house not made with hands,
Eternal in the heavens."

A Walking Tabernacle

The Mind
PROVERB 9:6 Leave your simple ways and you will live;
Walk in the way of understanding.

The Mind

The Mind is a holy place.
Be careful of what you allow in.
It's so easy to sit passively by
And let anything enter your dwelling.

Television, movies, books and advertisements
Fight for your attention.
There is an entire science dedicated
To feeding your mind's suspension.

So easily are we
Distracted to be
Occupied by trivial nonsense.

Who's got what
Who's with who
And Other superficial pretense.

If the most powerful tool
In the hand of the oppressor
Is the mind of the oppressed,

It's possible that you've
Been duped into
Believing what you see is best.

The lie continues
Successfully for a while
As we wade in self gratification.

But Yahweh has said
Under no uncertain terms
That everything be for His glorification.

Beloved, hear my voice
Don't turn these words aside.

The Mind is a sacred space.

Feed it with nutrients
Like prayer and positivism
Let nothing pollute that place.

Exercise your mind
With reading and study
Challenge your current beliefs.

Look at your life
Make an honest observation
Are your belief's giving you relief?

Challenge the norms
As Yashua did
When He walked the earth plane.

Let nothing separate you
From eternal life
No thought, no belief, no false doctrine.

My brethren, be sure
And listen now
Before it's eternally too late.

Don't let someone else's arrogance
Nor your ignorance
Determine your immortal fate.

So believe me when I say
That you must stop,
Look around and see.

The beginning of love
Is the renewing of the mind.
On Him alone your mind must be.

A Walking Tabernacle

The Heart
PROVERBS 17:3 Gold and silver are tested by fire, and
A person 's heart is tested by the **LORD**.

The Heart

At a steady pace it beats
Like the sound of a native drum.
An indication that life is present.

Still deeper into the heart we venture
Finding that there is
A much higher purpose there.

The heart-the mind's first cousin.
Virtual live-in companions.
What's in the mind, dwells in the heart.

No sin or disdainful act
Is committed with the physical heart.
The negative spirit
That dwells in the heart
That dwells in the mind
Animates the body
Commits the act.

"Whatever is in a man's heart
So shall it be manifested."

Clean heart
Right mind
Possible only
When the Holy Spirit is in the heart.

A Walking Tabernacle

The Ear
MATHEW 13:19 Those who hear the message about the Kingdom
But do not understand it are like the seeds that fell along the path.
The Evil one comes and snatches away what was sown in them.

The Ear

Those who have ears
      Let them hear
Let them hear what is true.

Those who have ears
      Let them hear
What Yah is trying to do.

Those who have ears
      Let them hear
For…He is close and near.

Those who have ears
      Let them hear
That God was always there.

Those who have ears
      Let them hear
He's with you everywhere.

Those who have ears
      Let them hear
That Yahweh is speaking a word
      Of truth that should be
Passed through you and me.

Messages To The Family

The Ties That Bind

Romans 12:10:

Be kindly affectionate one to another
With brotherly love; in honor
Preferring one another;

The Ties That Bind

Young Mother
TITUS 2:12 It teaches us to say " No" to ungodliness
And worldly passions, and to live self-controlled, upright
And godly lives in this present age.

Young Mother

The deed is done
The baby's here
What are you going to do?
Or have you thought about it, my dear?

What do you know about being a mom?
Not trying to put you down at all.
We all do things that we have to grow through.
And sweetheart, you done the thing.
It's time to grow.

Your baby is not your mama's
Or your grandma's
They didn't lay
You did.
They've raised their children.
Now it's time for you to raise yours.

Think about how you feel about your mom.
Whatever you do or don't like about her
She's yours.
And your child will feel the same way.
What legacy are you giving them about you?

Partying all night?
Laying still?
Baby comes last?
Well, you're in for a treat.
We've all done things we have to grow through.
You keep piling it on
You'll eventually have to grow or die.
I assume you don't want to do the latter
So go
Grow.

The responsibility lies with you.

Oh, yes that's a scary word.
You might as well face it now
Because, believe me you will have to.
Had you practiced maturity
Baby wouldn't be here just yet.

Ask an elder what you need to know
They'll be happy to show you how
And you can learn from them.
Young Mother.

The Ties That Bind

You
JAMES 1:23-24 For if any be a hearer of the word, and no doer,
He is like unto a man beholding his natural face in a glass.

For he behold himself and go his way , and straight way forget
What manner of man he was.

You

If the children would just act right
I wouldn't be so stressed out.

If the husband brings home more money
Then we'd be happier and closer.

If the wife cooks and cleans like she supposed
The I'd send her flowers.

If mom would let me stay out later
I wouldn't be so angry all the time.

If I got that raise
I could pay my bills.

If the people at my place of worship were nicer
I'd go more often.

If people weren't so mean
I'd speak to them.

If you focus more on internal
And less on the external
You
Will find
It's not the wife, husband, kids, job,
Not the church, school, or other people.
You are the problem.

The Ties That Bind

He, She, They
COLOSSIANS 3:2 For we are circumcision, which worship
God in the Spirit, and rejoice in Christ Jesus, and have no
Confidence in the flesh.

He, She, They

He was lost
She was found
She had the Spirit.
She obeyed her husband.
She worshipped and praised Yahweh.
She received
Many blessings for the Father.
She praised Yahweh for them.
She had all the things
She prayed for
But once the newness
Of her gifts wore off,
Little by little she turned away from Elohim.
She stopped seeking His face.
She fell stricken with great sickness.
Her limbs were not functioning well.
Her husband did all he could for her.
He gave his will to the Father.
And received the Holy Spirit.
He obeyed the Father.
He was blessed.
He worshipped Yahweh Elohim.
She became increasingly hostile.
She fought with her husband.
Her eyes were filled with hatred.
He continued to obey the Father.
He continued to read scripture.
He continued to praise the name of Yashua.
He continued to play spiritual music in the house.
He continued to love her.
He prayed for Yahweh mercy.
He prayed for his wife.
In the Father's time

After Patience had her perfect turn
She realized she never had the Holy Spirit
Once you have Him
He takes up permanent residence within you.
She was set free.
The two of them became one.
They worshipped Yahweh together.
United and connected were they in every way.
Their bond grew stronger.
They loved Yashua.
They loved each other.
They gave Yahweh all the glory.
He, she, and they were lovers once again.

The Ties That Bind

Admonishment To The Family

EPHESIANS 6:4 And ye fathers, provoke not your children to wrath,
But bring them up in the discipline and admonition of the Lord.

EPHESIANS 5:22 Wives, submit yourselves unto your own husbands,
As unto the Lord.

EPHESIANS 5:23 For the husband is the head of the wife, even as
Christ is the head of the church; and He is the Savior of the body.

EPHESIANS 5:25 Husbands, love your wives, even as Christ also
Loved the church, and gave Himself for it.

EPHESIANS 5:26 That He might sanctify and cleanse it with the
Washing of water by the word.

EPHESIANS 6:1 Children, obey your parents in the Lord for this
Right.

EPHESIANS 6:2 Honor thy father, mother, which is the first commandment
With promise.

EPHESIANS 6:3 That it may be well with thee, and thou may live long
On the earth.

Admonishment in the Family

Fathers be strong and meek in your house
These strange bedfellows can co-exist.
The challenge for you is to know
When to be which.

If your son wants to model his underwear,
Be strong.
It's disrespectful to everyone,
Including himself.

If your daughter stays out past dark,
Be strong.
The freaks come out at night
And day.
If she doesn't learn self-respect and modesty,
She becomes their prey.

If your wife's annoyed
Due to the seat's up position,
Be meek.
It's cold in them there hills.
And take this also to heart:
She may be the weaker vessel,
But she's not a punching bag
A sex toy
Or your personal maid and chef.
A strong leader knows from who is to take direction
Your wife is your help meet
Follow the pattern of God's love
And meet your obligations.
She is obliged to meet hers.

Mothers be strong and meek in your house.
These strange bedfellows can co-exist.
The challenge for you is to know,
When to be which.

If your little girl has suddenly become a woman,
Be strong.
Now is not the time to waste tears.
Be sure she is educated about her body.
About the difference between men and boys.
About self-respect and abstinence
And the sweet refuge of "no."
And when the time
Of her true womanhood arrives,
You'll cry tears of joy.

If you hear your son
Refer to a female as another species,
Pop him in the mouth.
It's a lewd, crude, utterly disgraceful thing
For anyone to deface the beauty that is woman.
Without her, no man could be here.
And the world would be void.

Brothers and sisters
These two can also co-exist.
Your sister can give you advice
About what attracts ladies.
Your brother can give you the low-down
On what young men find comely.
This attraction is a natural thing.
But be responsible.
Listen to what good sense sounds like:
If you're sneaking to do it,
It isn't right.
Be the opposite of what Nike says,
And just don't do it.

If your husband is annoyed,
Due to the seat's down position
Be meek.
He's allowed, too.
When you know he's led by God,

Respect his leadership.
God knows something you don't
Because he put man in charge.
You may be able to do everything he does
And particularly not in public.
Have eyes only for him and ears too.
Just like in days past,
Listening to the charms of lesser man
Can create a world of trouble.

Now this is most important of all:
Know the truth about God.
He is the ultimate Source and Substance
Of all things.
"They that worship him, must worship him
In spirit and in truth."
Truth simply is.
God Is.
"And this is life eternal,
That they might know thee
The only true El
And Yashua the Messiah,
Whom Thou has sent."

Don't be afraid to be Father in your house.
Don't be fearful of being Mother in your house.
You are the boss.
Not your children.
You provide for them.
They don't take care of you.
Be strong and be meek your house!

Demystify the Creator and know Him
Before it's eternally too late.
Know Him as intimately
As He knows you.
This is eternal life.

The Ties That Bind

Generation neXt
PROVERBS 3:11-12 My son, despise not the chastening of the LORD;
Neither be weary of His correction.

For whom the LORD love He correct; even as a Father the son
In whom he delight.

Generation neXt

Hey generation Eerrs!
Let me holler at yaw a few ticks.
I've got a secret to tell
About what you're doing to get your kicks.

Are you sneaking around
Hanging uptown
Smoking a little herb?
Or messing around
 And sleeping around
With a bunch of boys or girls?

Listen a minute
Don't be shocked
By my straightforward words.
I've been where you are;
This advice doesn't come
From something I've just heard.

Smoking herb and
Hooking school
And playing doctors and nurse,
May seem real cool
And feel real good
But these days, doing "it"
Can land you in a hearse.

Now, I know you know
You've got all the answers
And grown-ups are really out of touch.
But, look, slow down
For one moment or two
And just pretend you don't know so much.

With protection you think
You'll be okay

So you go ahead and do the do
But it's not just a baby
Or an incurable disease
That'll make a mess of you.

It's the disgust you'll feel
And the shame you'll face
When you come to realize

Playing grown up
And thinking you'll be fine
Was all a part of the disguise.
To pacify you
And feed your desires
That amount to absolutely nothing.

So you can't see the Way
Your too busy with play
To see the unspeakable blessing.
Of knowing your Creator
And understanding His existence
And that you are merely a vessel.

There's a spirit in you
That's animates that body
It's either good or bad.
If you're smoking herb
And hooking school,
You better check which one you have.

Do it now
In this day and age
Before it's eternally too late.
Give yourself half a chance
Take an original stance
A powerful prerequisite trait.

Ask questions

Demand answers
For things you can't understand.
If your pastor or mother
Or trusted friend
Can't satisfy
Take heart
You haven't reach your end.

Simply pray for the Spirit
And that God have mercy
And that He show you the true way.

Some way, somehow
If you earnestly seek
Be diligent about knowing Him.
He's not some ghost in the air
Up in the sky.
He'll show you what you need.

When you come of wisdom
Not particularly age.
You'll understand what I say.
The devil is alive
And active as hell
Seeking to destroy who he may.
Sex, drugs and violence
Is the disguise.
That keeps shut your seeing eyes.
Think for yourself.

The Ties That Bind

Greet One Another
PROVERBS 16:24 Pleasant words are as an honey comb, sweet to the Soul, and health to the bones.

Greet One Another

Do you greet one another with a kiss?
Or do you roll up your sleeves
And ball up your fist?

Confront one another with a kind hello.
Oh, by the way, how was your day?

These days it is rare
To show that you care.

But defy the norms
A smile to another
Be ready to share.

Use low soft talk
And not a loud yell.

Be sweet and cooperative
From kindness don't rebel.

Hey, you know what I mean.
Don't be so disturbing.

Greet one another
With cheerful words.

Your kindness to a stranger or neighbor
To others might be transferred.

The Ties That Bind

Big Kids
PROVERBS 29:17 Correct thy son, and he shall give thee rest; yea
He shall give delight unto thy soul.

Big Kids

So you want to grow up
And be on your own.
You think it will make you independent
So nobody tells you what to do.

You can go out when you want.
Eat what you want.
You'll have money to buy what you want.
And no one will be the boss of you.
Because you're a grown-up
Is real hard work.
And I know you don't like work
Especially the kind that's hard

Moms and dads are like circus jugglers
They keep so many balls in the air
Careful not to let any of them fall.
Work, bills, you, house.
And some even have a ball for school up there.

So don't be in such a hurry
To be all grown up
Play games with your friends.
Laugh for no reason.
Sing and dance around the house.
Be a kid.

There may come a time
When you'll be sorry these days are gone.

The Ties That Bind

Little Children
PROVERBS 17:6 Children's children are the crown of old men, and the Glory of children are their fathers.

EPHESIANS 5:1 Be ye therefore followers of God, as dear children.

Little Children

Come on, little children
Add and count with me
Let's make it fun.

I'll tell you a little secret
When our counting done.

One and one
Equal two.

Someone's special
And it's you.

Two and two
Equal four.

God, help us grown-ups
To love and treasure you more.

Three plus three
Equal six.

I love the crayon colors
You mix.

Four and four
Equal eight.

Eat all the green beans
From off your dinner plate.

Five plus five
Equal ten.

Now I'll tell you a secret
Grown-ups want to be like you again!

The Ties That Bind

A Product Of Me
GENESIS 1:27 So God created man in His own image, in the image of God He him; male and female created he them.

A Product Of Me

Do you want a child
Who's cute, cuddly and sweat?

So you can say
He or she is a product of me?

Do you want a child
Who's respectful in every way?

So you can say
That's a product of me?

Do you want a child
That gets A's and B's on his report card?

So you can say
That's a product of me?

When that child gets out of hand.
Can you still say
That's a product of me?

Or do you say that child is just like
His mother or father?

Why is that when a child
Is doing well,
You say that's a product of me?

But when a child begins
To act out
You can't say that.

Listen,
A child is a product of you.
Whether good or bad.

You are a product
Of your Creator
Each day you live
He lets you breathe the air
He made,
Whether you've been good or
Bad.
Now what can you say?

The Ties That Bind

Mother
2CORINTHIANS 8:14 But by equality, that now at this time your abundance may be a supply for their want, that their abundance also may be equality.

Mother

You are my Mother
Knowing just when to cover.
I remember when you said
I will be the Mother.
And ask God to be the Father
The two of you together
Kept well me, my sisters
 And my brother.

If one strayed away.
God was always behind.
He was my Father.
And you, my Mother.
His sweet spirit has been
Deposited in you.

You birth His spirit
Every time you gave
Of yourself to so many.

The marriage yet continues
He is still blessing you._____

The Ties That Bind

She
GENSIS 1:1 In the beginning God created the heavens and the earth.

PSALMS 147:15 He send forth His commandment upon earth! His Word run very swiftly.

She

She was going on vacation.
In another city.
Cozy little town.
Just north of Mississippi.

Got there as the sun went down.
Even in this small place,
She could see
The beauty
The magnificence
Of the Creator

Brilliance of the descending light
Holds momentarily in its embrace
A sight so glorious
It can only be
Described in silence…

The cool, evening breeze
Tickle the pansies
Their wiggles give away
Their laughter.

Their elders look down
With adoration.
Their many arms raised
In never ending praises.

She smiles as she wipes
Her grateful tears away.
No matter where she goes
His finger is there.
So picturesque is His handiwork
His signature on all His art.

The Ties That Bind

Sisters
JOHN 13:34 A new commandment I give unto you, that ye love one Another, as I have loved you, that ye also love one another.

Sisters

It was a Friday night.
The sisters were gather together
For a sleep over.
They all sat down on the floor
Sitting Indian style.
The sisters were facing each other,
While holding hands, sharing concerns,
And casting their cares.

Sisters are the one who always
Show the willingness of being there.
It's a joy to have sisters who can
Share the laughter of reminiscing about,
When we were little children.

As for having sisters we can always
Go back and remember the times,
When we helped one another.

It's that love that we share for each other.
It's a joy to have you as sisters
The one who's always there,
Sharing your concerns and casting cares.

Thank you sisters for being there.
Sisters God has given us the responsibility
For looking out for one another.
Cast your cares openly sisters with your
Love, concerns, and willingness to be there.

Sisters thank you for showing that you care.
For we may have many more sleepovers.
In the coming years.
Just bring yourself,
Your love
Your concerns

Your cares
And prayers.

The Ties That Bind

Daughter
PSALM 66:11 The Lord gave the command, and many woman carried
The news;

Daughter

There was an echo coming from the hill top.
A sound that echo,
Daughter, daughter, daughter.
The sound echo three times again,
Daughter, daughter, daughter.

It was coming from the hill top.
A sound that echo ,
Daughter, daughter, daughter.
It was three times again.

"Daughter, daughter, daughter, pay attention!"
So she remained still.
Then she listen closely.

This echoing sound that you are hearing
Is coming from within .
"Daughter, daughter, daughter, pay attention!"
As she began to concentrate.
The room was silent.

Then she listen tentatively again.
Focusing not on herself,
But the sound that was calling her from within.

Now that the spirit have you still.
The sound that you were hearing, is Yahweh
Who want You
       To
         Be
           Still
             And
               To
                 Do
                   His
                     Will.

The Ties That Bind

Big Brother
REVELATION 3:20 Listen! I stand at the door and knock; if anyone hears
My voice and opens the door, I will come into his home and he will eat
With Me.

Big Brother

I sat on my steps with the ball, and mitt in my hand.
Then I began wondering , only if I had someone to
Pitch, catch, and play ball with.

Oh, how I began to pray.
If only, if only I had One Who is like a Father
That would come my way.

I saw a Man who came my way.
He looked just like me.
He asked a question?
Could I play catch with you?

I smiled at Him.
I knew that my prayers had been answered.
God had sent me a Big Brother.
One who looked just like me.
One who was able to help me
In the time of disparity.

This Man saw the look on my face.
He heard my heart.
As I touched His heart.
He stepped right on in.
He was not only my Big Brother, Father,
But a good Friend.
He showed me how to pitch and catch.
And He never complained at all.

"He said to me, the next day, I will show you
How to play basketball!"
Maybe the next time we could run a little track.
After that day is through,
I pray that you will call
Me back.

I Am very easily to be reach.
Just continue to pray.
As you have done before.
And I will be the One Who's
Standing at the door.
So continue to open up the
Door of your heart.
And speak Me into existence.

For I Am all that you need
Me to be.
Your Father,
Big Brother
Friend
And Teacher
Get into the habit to
Know the Door Keeper.

The Ties That Bind

Son
ROMANS 2:10 But God will give glory, honor, and peace to all who do
What is good, to the Jews first and also to the Gentiles.

Son

This is my son.
The precious little one.
When he was only one years of age.
I can remember him playing
With his building blocks.

His hands was the hand of a carpenter.
The steadiness that I saw in his eyes.
I knew that he was going to be an architect.

Then as my son grew older.
I had plans ready for him.
I made telephone calls to all my friends
Telling them that my son is going to
School for architect.

Yes he's going to do architect
And I told everyone.
"My son is going to school for architect!"

This particular day my son came to me
"He said, Mommy did you ask me
What I wanted to be?"
It seems that you have the plans for
My future, all wrap up for me.
But I have something to tell you.

Last night I had a dream
And in this dream it was a word
From the Most High.
He spoke to me.
Whatever I wanted to be
I will be; but do remember Me.

So Mommy in this dream
Yahweh was speaking to me.

My son what-ever you're going
To be you will be
Do know your Father
Will be well please.
And thank you for reverencing Me.

Mommy excuse me,
For I don't want to sound
Disrespectful .
But Yahweh is first in my life.
And He comes before anyone.
I will still be your son
For I know what
I want to become.
Yahweh is the **Only One Who**
Holds the plans, for my
Future
Purpose
And Destiny.

Mommy, I will still be your son,
With the hands of a carpenter
That designs like an architect
And your precious little one.

Warning and Admonishment

The Trumpet's Growl

Isaiah 58:1:

Cry aloud, spare not, lift up thy voice
Like a **trumpet**, and show my people
Their transgression, and the house of
Jacob their sins.

The Trumpets Growl

Observations of the Human Conditions

ISAIAH 6:9-10 He said, "Go and tell this people: be ever hearing
Never understanding; be ever seeing, but never perceiving.

Make their ears dull and close their eyes. "Otherwise they might see
With their eyes, hear with their ears, understand with their hearts,
And turn and be healed."

Observation of the Human Condition

From a natural point of view
There isn't much to see.
We know what the problems are,
Our apathy just lets it be.

Everybody's trying to appease everybody
And no one is pleased.
Everybody's want to do their thing
And wants somebody else to say, "It's okay."

Well, it's not okay!
Can you honestly look around
And proclaim satisfaction with our world?

Country against country
Race against race
Men against women.
Mothers against daughters.
Sons against fathers.
Profilers versus pro-choicer.
Punishment versus rehabilitation.
Democrats versus Republicans.
Gay versus Straight.
Defense above education.
Man's insatiable thirst
For power, position, and profit
At the expense of,
The world's morality
The children's innocence
And the earth's beauty.

For what?
Progression of civilization?
What a crock?
Everything we see
Hear

Taste
Touch, and
In many cases,
Smell and
Feel,
Has been manufactured
For the purpose of
Personal profit or power
Not because of a deep-seated
Moral obligation
To advanced the human condition.
So we do nothing?

When will we truly stand
And do what we know is right?
Not politically correct
Or socially acceptable
Just down right, good common sense.

"If my people, which are called by name,
Shall humble themselves, and pray,
And seek My face,
And turn from their wicked ways;
Then will I hear from heaven,
And will forgive their sin,
And will heal their land."

Given the human condition,
This makes the most sense.

The trumpets Growl

Do You Know Where We're Going
PROVERBS 16:2 All a man's ways seem innocent to him.

PROVERBS 16:8 Better a little with righteousness than gain with Injustice.

PROVERBS 16:9 In his heart a man plans his course, but the LORD Determines his steps.

Do You Know Where We're Going?

Stop blaming because of yesterday.
Your outrage is outrageous.
And it won't change
The unchangeable.

Those who are economically blessed
Bless those who are not.
Guard your beautiful children
With intense selfishness.
Teach them about them.
If others won't treat you right.
What makes you think, they'll teach you right?
Self-knowledge and self-acceptance
Are the beginning of
All wisdom and universal love.

America: Lynn Johnston said,
"An apology is the superglue of life.
It can repair just about anything."
You are a superpower.
You have the influence, respect and prestige.
Do you have the courage, the conviction
Or the character?
To make things right
When things are so wrong?

You may be a superpower
But you are not The Superpower.
And every man **must** give an account.
What have you deposited in your spiritual bank?

The eve of the millennium is come
Do we know where we're going?
As a people
As a community
As a country

Can we see the variations of beauty
The electric rays of sun
The myriad of flowers that bloom.
What will you do
And what will I do
Heightened hate says
We must act soon.

Fair gains and equal access
Is everyone's right
There should be no movement
For these inalienable things
We must move forward
And upward
And onward
This should be our direction

Because if we don't know
Where we're going
We'll go where we're headed.

The Trumpets Growl

The Peacemaker
REVELATION 11:15-19 The seventh angel sounded his trumpet, and their
Were loud voices in heaven, which said; " The kingdom of the world has
Become the kingdom of our Lord and His Christ and He will reign forever
And ever."

And the twenty-four elders, who were seated, on their thrones before God
Fell on their faces and worshiped God.

Saying: "We give thanks to you, Lord God Almighty, the One Who is
And Who was, because You have taken Your great power and have began
To reign.

The nations were angry; and Your wrath has come, the time has come for
Judging the dead and for rewarding Your servants the prophets, and Your
Saints and those who reverence Your name, both small and great and for
Destroying those who destroy the earth.

The God's temple in heaven was opened, and within His temple was seen
The ark of His covenant, and there came flashes of lightning, rumbling,
Peals of thunder, an earthquake and great hail storm.

ISAIAH 44:6 " This is what the Lord says Israel's King and Redeemer
That Lord Almighty: I Am the First and I Am the Last; apart from Me
There is no God.

ISAIAH 44:7 Who is like Me? Let him proclaim it. Let him declare
And lay out before Me, what has happened since I established my ancient
People, and what is yet to come-yes, let him foretell what will come.

ISAIAH 44:8 Do not tremble, do not be afraid. Did I not proclaim this
And foretell it long ago? You are my witness. Is there any God besides Me?

The Peacemaker

We think of the Messiah
Coming in white raiment.
Halo shining above
His brilliant crown.

Soft, gentle face
Speaking loving, kind words.
He is a peacemaker.
This is what we think
When we think of the Messiah.

Come to save the world.
Come to spread, joy, peace and love.
Everything good.
Everyone happy.
To sit at His feet
And be loved.

Feeding the multitudes
Healing the sick
Taming the crazed.
This is what we think
When we think of the Messiah
The Peacemaker.

Listen to His words
As He commands
Through His disciple Mathew:
"Think not that I Am come
To send peace on earth:
I came not to send peace,
But a sword."

How accustomed are we
To gravitate toward His love
Never to consider

His smoldering wrath.

On His mercy we depend
To be our saving grace
Lest we get a notion
To assume responsibility
For being a participant
In His grace.

Only the Messiah is able
To strike a perfect balance
In His peace
In His wrath
In His justice.
A mighty, powerful hand
Is His sword.

Consider again His words
Through Luke
Another of His disciple,
And examine where you are
In his plot:
"Suppose ye that I Am come
To give peace on earth?
I tell you Nay:
But rather division."

Too often we hear
But ignore the trumpets.

The Trumpets Growl

Never Entertain The Devil
REVELATION 16:14 They are spirits of demons performing miracles
Signs, and they go out to the kings of the whole world, to gather them
For the battle on the great day of God Almighty.

Never Entertain The Devil

Never entertain the devil.
His wrap is lame.
He has no manners.
He comes to the door smelling.
Never bathed, you see.

Never entertain the devil.
Even if he brings soup
It's the same soup
Just a different day.
His tastes are the same, you see.

Never entertain the devil
Don't call him for tea.
He never does what is proper.
He gulps down the goodies
And speaks out of turn.
He's a beast.
Never been to obedience school, you see.

Even with this warning
I know you will
Still
Entertain the devil
'Cause he's smooth
Like old Bill.

Looks real good
Hiding His true identity.
Scent smells so nice
Without a spiritual sniff.
And he'll behave
At first.

By the time you see
The maggots

Gnats
And flies,
He'll be
Laughing,
Having a good old time
He's prankster, too, you see.
He entertains himself.

The Trumpets Growl

Closing The Door

MATHEW 25: 10-13 "But while they were on their way to buy the oil
The Bridegroom arrived. The virgins who were ready went in with Him
For the wedding banquet. And the door was shut.

"Later the others also came, 'Sir! Sir! They said. "Open the door for us!"

"But He replied, " I tell you the truth, I don't know you."

"Therefore keep watch, because you do not know the day or the hour.

Closing The Door

He's closing the door
On this Age.
As in the days of Noah
He's closing the door.

He's closing the door
Can't you hear the trumpets blasting?
As in the days of Noah
He's closing the door.

Behind the closed door
In the land of Egypt
The lamb in them
Those were spared
The wrath of the Father.

Once the door is closed
No one can get in
Can't you hear the trumpets blasting?
Run, don't walk
To the feet of the Lamb
Beg for His mercy.
As in the days of Noah,
He's closing the door.

The Trumpets Growl

Never Before
HEBREW 4:12 For the Word of God is living and active. Sharper than any
Double-edged sword, it penetrates even to dividing soul and spirit, joints
And marrow; it judges the thoughts and attitudes of the heart.

HEBREW 4:13 Nothing in all creation is hidden from God's sight. Everything
is uncovered and laid bare before the eyes of Him to whom
We must give account.

Never Before

Never before have we seen
Nor encountered the atrocities of today
That plaque our land and the world
Bringing upon us much dismay.

Children killing children
For reason unknown
Mayhem all around
Surely we reap what we have sown.

We propagate "isms" and hate
And that is what we breed
We teach money is everything
Ere a TV show called **Greed**.

We promote self-idolatry
Through media and films
Supporting its okay
To placate our slightest whims.

Even our songs sing a deadly tune
Of deceit, hate and lust
Never before have lyrics summoned
From some such a level of disgust.

Are we content to be one day saddened
By the world's condition
The next day trudging along in apathy
Or will these words be ammunition.

To fall on your knees
Beg for mercy and plead for
A delay of justified reprisal

To admit gratifying our lusts
Have ushered in our destruction

And beckoned His despisal .

Chaos covers us like a blanket
Warning our desires.
But never before have we imagined
The burn felt from the fire.

The day of reckoning will surely come
Give an ear to the trumpets growl
No man knows when He will come
Not the day nor the hour.

The Trumpets Growl

Confusion

ROMANS 1:20 For since the creation of the world God's invisible qualities
His eternal power and divine nature-have been clearly seen, being
Understood from what has been made, so that men are without excuse.

ROMANS 1:21 For although they knew God, they neither glorified Him as
God nor gave thanks to Him, but their thinking became futile and their
Foolish hearts were darkened.

ROMANS 1:22 Although they claimed to be wise, they became fools.

ROMANS 1:23 And exchanged the glory of the immortal God for images
Made to look like mortal man and birds and animals and reptiles.

ROMANS 1:24 Therefore God gave them over in the sinful desires of their
Hearts to sexual impurity for the degrading of their bodies with one another.

ROMANS 1:25 They exchanged the truth of God for a lie, and worshiped
And served created things rather than the Creator- who is forever praised.
Amen.

ROMANS 1:26 Because of this, God gave them over to shameful lusts. Even
their women exchanged natural relations for unnatural ones.

ROMANS 1:27 In the same way the men also abandoned natural relations
With women and were inflamed with lust for one another. Men committed
Indecent acts with other men, and received in themselves the due penalty
For their perversion.

ROMANS 1:28 Furthermore, since they did not think it worthwhile to retain
The knowledge of God, He gave them over to a depraved mind, to do what
Ought not to be done.

MATHEW 4:13 Nothing in all creation is hidden from God's sight. Everything
is uncovered and laid bare before the eyes of Him to whom
We must give account.

REVELATION 22:14-16 Blessed are those who wash their robes, that
They may have the right to the tree of life and may go through the gates
Into the city.

Outside are dogs, those who practice magic arts, the sexually immoral,
The murderers, the idolaters and everyone who loves and practice falsehood.

I, Jesus have sent my angel to give you this testimony for the churches, I Am
The Root and the Offspring of David, and the bright Morning Star.

Confusion

Men you are the image of God.
You are formed in His likeness
He has given you dominion
Over all the earth.

Confusion is man with man.
It's not the will of the Father.
It's the will of man.
Woman you are a helper
Suitable for man.

Confusion woman with woman.
It's not the will of the Father.
It's the will of woman.
Look at the picture.
Examine yourself closely.
Then what is it that you see.
Is it Confusion?

Let's be clear.
Every instance in scripture
That speaks on the topic
Talks of the abomination it is
In the sight of the Father .

Men and women
We are His bride
We have an inherent desire
For the Bridegroom.
We confuse this
With same sex lust.

Any justification or rationale
Is based on the ego
And its desire to persist
In its own gratification.

No matter how perverse.

The Father has spoken.
Will you ignore Him?
No need to fuss or make
Ruckus about tolerance
And the right to exercise
Preferences.

The bridegroom is coming
And he's coming for His
Bride.
Not one who practices
spiritual adultery.

The Trumpets Growl

Light or Dark
LUKE 11:33 "No one lights a lamp and puts it in a place where it will be
Hidden, or under a bowl. Instead he puts it on it's stand, so that those who
Come in may see the light.

LUKE 11:34 Your eyes is the lamp of your body. When your eyes are
Good, your whole body also is full of light. But when they are bad, your
Body also full of darkness.

LUKE 11:35 Therefore be careful lest the light in you be darkness.

Light or Dark

The greatest opposers
There is not one without the other
Light brings
Vision
Clarity
Direction.

Darkness blinds
Clouds
Obstructs.

Light is synonymous with
Peace
Calm
Certainty.

Darkness is associated with
Anxiety
Fright
Confusion

"If thy whole body therefore be full of light,
Having no part dark, the whole shall be
Full of light, as when the bright shining
Of a candle doth give thee light."

"But the children of the kingdom
Shall be cast out into outer darkness:
There shall be weeping
And gnashing of teeth."

Choose this day
Where you'd rather be.
In the Light or
In the Dark.

The Trumpets Growl

What the World Needs
MARK 9:50 "Salt is good, but if it loses it's salt ness, How can you
Make it salty again? "Have salt in yourselves and be at peace with
Each other.

What the World Needs

What the world needs
   Is joy.
What the world needs
   Is love.
What the world needs
   Is peace.
What the world needs
   Is joy, love, unity, peace.

Yashua brings joy.
Gives love.
Breeds peace.
Is unity.

What the world needs
Is the belief that Yashua
Brings joy that can't be corrupted.

What the world needs
Is belief in sacred words
That tell of a love so great,
A man would lay down his life.

What the world needs
Is belief in the possibility
That differences can be respected.
God, the Word, and The Holy Spirit
These three are One.
A unity.

What the world needs,
Is a belief that it needs.
When we admit our inability
To even breathe without
The indescribable power
Of the Creator
Then we will inherit peace..

The Trumpets Growl

Deal With It
MATHEW 16:24 Then Yashua / Jesus said to His disciples. "If anyone
Would come after Me, he must deny himself and take up his cross and
Follow Me.

Deal With It

An unfriendly neighbor
      A racist
A wayward child
      A drug user
No money in the bank
      Bills are due
No raise this year
      Falling heath
Torn relationships
      Chaos and disorder
Looked over for a promotion
      Scarcity everywhere

If any of these is your current plight,
      Deal with it.

Harsh though it may seem,
      It is up to you
      To stop the whining.

Everyone's going thru something
      You are not unique.

The only One that has power to
      Make the wrongs right
      Straighten the crooked
      Clear the path
      Calm the raging sea
      Is Yashua the Messiah.

Newsflash: Without Him
      You **are** nothing
      Can do nothing
      Be nothing
      Fix nothing

Get Him
And just deal with it.

The Trumpets Growl

Ever Wonder Why?
PSALM 95:I7 For He is our God and we are the people of
His pastures the flock under His care.

ISIAH 40:11 He tends Hid flock like a Shepherd: He gathers
The lambs in His arms and carries them close to His heart;
He gently leads those that have young.

Ever Wonder Why?

We're here
In this place
At this time.
Why?
Ever Wonder?

Your life
Can be on an upswing
And then for no apparent reason
Down again.
Why?
Ever Wonder?

Some people
Are born privileged
Some people
Are born to destitution.
Why?
Ever Wonder?

The world appears to be
In chaos
Lawlessness
Confusion
Why?
Where are we headed?
Ever Wonder?

These among many questions
Plague the human mind
The Answer:
Everything exists
Inside Yahweh plan.

He created us
Because it pleased Him.

He created time and eternity.
A day is as one thousand years
To Yahweh.
He created the Heavens and Earth.
He saw that it was good.

He created seasons for earth
And for life
Your life
Ups and downs:
They are and always will be.

He created good
He created evil.
I bet that's something
You never heard the preacher say.
But It's clearly written
In the Book.
Just take a look.

He has allowed the adversary
To have reign over the world
And as you can tell
He's doing a bang up job.

The adversary feeds off division:
Racism
Class-ism
Sexism
Anything that's
A better-than you-ism.
Our vanity
Has us locked in a death trap.
Unable to see
Past me.

But it's not all about you.
It's all about Him.

Yashua can loose
The shackles that bind.
That keeps us wondering
why.
He is the Answer
To every imaginable
question.
Know Him and know
the answer.
For this is eternal life.

Everything that is
That happens
That can be Points to Yahweh.

The Trumpets Growl

Ignorance and Arrogance
MATHEW 7:13-14 "Enter through the narrow gate. For wide is the gate
And broad is the road that leads to destruction, and many enter through it.

But small is the gate and narrow the road that leads to life, and only a few
Find it.

MATHEW 22:14 "For many are invited, but few are chosen."

PROVERB 4:26 Plan carefully what you do, and whatever you do will
Turn out right.

Ignorance and Arrogance

Ignorance and Arrogance
Strange bedfellows they are not.
Both are from the same family.
Although Arrogance would argue they're not.

The two are commonly seen
Strolling elbow in elbow down the block
Ignorance, head hung low
While Arrogance glides,
Proud as a peacock.

The pair set out
To go to church one day
But not before arguing
Which way was the right way.

Arrogance, tongue so well-practiced
Words so smooth and sure
Won the spat hands down.
Making Ignorance all the more insecure.

Led by Arrogance
They walked swiftly down Humble St.
Made a left on Modest Lane
And then a right on Meek Peak.

All was going well
Their steps seemed straight
Until they reached a dead end.
To which Ignorance mocked,
"That's just great!"

Before Arrogance could speak
Ignorance did an about face.
Arrogance followed reluctantly behind him.
To take the lead again

Just in case.

Ignorance hung a left on Investi Gate
Then turned right on Knowl Edge.
Straight past Wise Lane
Just one block short
Of Understanding Ledge.

Suddenly he stopped
And looked both ways.
Then scratched his head.
Because he'd led them into
 A big, confusing maze.

Never to the church
Did the pair arrive.
Some say they see the two
Near Old Man Lucifer's lake.
As they drive by.

At the start of their trip
Both were sure
Their way was right
But for all their fervent bickering,
Both are but lost ships in the night.

Arrogance goes around town
Pretending he knows.
But there's proof he doesn't.
He just deeps it on the down low.

He couldn't find his way
Because he does not recognize
Modesty, Meekness, and Humility.
He just has his eye on one thing:
His own self-glorified prize.

Ignorance can't see the way

172

Because he's fighting or following Arrogance;
If he'd Investigate on his own
And gain some knowledge for himself
His reward would be understanding and wisdom
And not a brain abandoned on the shelf.

There is no excuse for anyone
Not to find The Way.
The direction lie all around us.
We see it each and every day.

Take off the blinders
Unstop your ears
Be humble not arrogant
Yours could be eternal years.

Let no man deceive you.
In this world he does it everyday.
With bright lights and fancy signs
Arrogance and Ignorance
Points to a way that seems okay.

But, alas, we are ultimately accountable
This mistake do not make
Be sure you are not spotted
Anywhere near Lucifer's lake.

The Trumpets Growl

Scars
ISAIAH 52:14 Just as there were many who were appalled at Him, His
Appearance was so disfigured beyond that of any man, and His form
Marred beyond human likeness.

Scars

The **Scars** that can't be erase.
The **Scars** that were hidden in it's innermost place.
The **Scars** could no longer stay in.
Then the **Scars** surface upon the face.

The **Scars** were black and blue.
The **Scars** waited patiently for someone to ask,
What happened to you?

The **Scars** had it shares of,
The **Lashes**,
The **Whips**,
The **Pain**
That violated the innocent.

The **Scars** cried from out, can someone see?
The **Scars** that said, "Please don't pass me!"
The **Scars** which echoed for **Mercy**!
Could someone please help me?
Do not pass me by.
Just hear my cry's that echoed **Why? Why?**

The Trumpets Growl

Mastering What's In You

ISAIAH 1:19 If you are willing and obedient, you will eat the best from the Land.

ISAIAH 1:20 But if you resist and rebel, you will be devoured by the sword. "For the mouth of the Lord has spoken.

Mastering What's In You

Yahweh said to Cain,
Sin is knocking at your door.
You must master it,
But Cain kept on walking.
Anger was stored up in his heart.
Cain did an evil thing.

Yahweh has been watching him all that
day.
Yahweh began to speak to Cain.
"Cain where is your brother?"
Can answered, I'm I my brother's
keeper.

"Yahweh, said to Cain your brother's,
Blood cried out to Me from the ground."
Did you think that you were going to
escape?

I have told you from the beginning.
"Sin is knocking at your door,
But you must master it."
Cain you have done an evil thing.

Now the curse has fallen on you.
When you walk on the face of the earth,
Your conscience will bother you.
If any man touches you, the same will
fall on him.

The circle goes around and around.
The same will fall on you.
What goes around comes around.
Control your temper,
Before your temper,
Takes control of you.

Learn from what Cain did to Abel,
And don't let this happen to you.
Control your temper,
Before your temper,
Takes control over you.

You must be the one to master it.
Don't let the evil master you.
Learn from what Cain did to Abel.

The circle goes around and around.
The same will fall on you.
Control your temper,
Before your temper control you.
Learn from what Cain did to Abel.
Don't let this happened to you.

Yahweh already knows what's in the
heart.
Don't let this darkness enter you.
Learn from what Cain did to Abel.
Don't let it happened to you.

You must be to one to master it,
Or the evil will master you.
Learn from what Cain did to Abel.
Don't let your temper take control of
you.

The Trumpets Growl

Receive Me
ISAIAH 52:6 Therefore my people will know my name. Therefore in that
Day they will know that it is I who foretold it. Yes, it is I.

ISAIAH 52:10 The Lord will lay bare His holy arm in the sight of all the
Nations, and the ends of the earth will see the salvation of our God.

ZECHARIAH 2:13 Be still before the Lord, all mankind, because He has
Roused Himself from His holy dwelling.

JOHN 14:20 On that day you will realize that I am in my Father, and you
Are in me, and I am in you.

ISAIAH 52:15 So will He sprinkle many nations, and kings will shut their
Mouths because of Him. For what they were not told, they have not heard,
They will understand.

Receive Me

When **I** come again.
How would you receive **Me**?
Would you hide your face?
Will you know **Who I Am**?

Would you hide **Me** in your heart?
Will your lips be sealed?
Would your eyes be in awe at **Me**?

Will you say **Who** is that?
Would you hide behind a rock?
Will you be in shock?

Why should that be?
I have been here before.
I created the Universe,
And everything in it.

I called you out of Egypt.
I said to **Moses, I Am that I Am**.

I Am sent you.
I came to you as **Myself**.
I walked with you.
I sent you the **Comforter**.

He will show you.
How to worship **Me**,
Worship **Me** in **Spirit and in Truth**.

"But your rather listen, and give your praises to man."

I said to **Joshua**.
"Take them into the promise land!"
I Am still **I Am**.
The **One Who** knows all things.

The praises are on your lips.
So where is your heart?

When **he** came in **His Father's name**.
You received **him** not.
When **he** come again.
In **his Father's name**.
Would you do it to **him** again?

He was with **Me** since the foundation of this world.
Have it then your way, is it for your own self glorification?

Would you share **Us** with the world.
I Am the same yesterday, today, and forever.
My words never return back to Me void.
It's your unfaithfulness that will return.

Those who love **Me**
Let them worship **Me** in **Spirit and in Truth**.
I Am the First, and the Last,
I Am the Alpha and Omega,
The Beginning, and the End,
Who is equal to Me? No one.
I know all things, even what **I** have deposit inside of you.

I Am that I Am
The **One Who** formed you.
Will you share **Me** with others?
Or would you do to others, as you have done to **Me**?
"Really Have You Receive Me?"

The Trumpets Growl

Contagious

2CORINTHIANS 6:2 For He says, " In the time of my favor I heard you, And in the day of salvation I helped you." I tell you, now is the time of God's favor, now is the day of salvation.

REVELATION 12:10 " Then I heard a loud voice in heaven say: "Now Have come the salvation and power and the kingdom of our God, and the Authority of His Christ.
For the accuser of our brothers, who accuses them before our God day and Night has been hurled down.

REVELATION 19:1 After this I heard what sounded like the roar of a great Multitude in heaven shouting:
"Hallelujah! Salvation and glory and power belong to our God.

REVELATION 22:13 I Am the Alpha and the Omega, the First and the Last, the Beginning and the End.

REVELATION 22:16 " I Yashua Jesus, have sent my angel to give you this Testimony for the churches, I Am the Root and the Offspring of David, and The bright Morning Star.

MATHEW 22:44 " The Lord said to my Lord; Sit here at my side until I put Your enemies under your feet."

Contagious

There is a disease that is flowing around
From country to country.
If you stay around it much longer
It becomes contagious.
Keep on looking at the attitudes
That one betray, their acts are so outrageous.

Stay around just a little longer.
And it will become contagious.
They say it started from country to country.
Never looking inside of themselves.
Passing down the bigotry and self hatred.
From generation to generation.

Teaching one to hold up it's legacy.
Passing it on and on
Never let this chain be broken.

Running to and fro,
And joining every kind of organization.
Looking for answers,
From every kind of flesh.

Never taking the time to look up to the sky
To the **One Who** knows what's best.
Never falling on our knees to pray.
Until drama comes this way.
Then we remember the cross.

For He stands at the door of our hearts
And waiting patiently.
Giving us the answers, but one may never stop
And began to ask the question?

As long as flesh continue to over ride the spirit.
The spirit within sits on the side.

When we come from out of ourselves,
And allow Him to do His will.
Plug our-self into Him
And know **Who** is in control.

For someday we may walk into the enemy camp
And may become his prey.
But remember Genesis 3:14
Then the LORD God said to the snake,
"You will be punished for this, you alone of
all the animals must bear this curse:
From now on you will crawl on your belly,
And you will have to eat dust as long as
You live.

As you go on search a little further.
Remember Revelation 12:12-13 .
And so be glad, you heavens, and all you
That live there! But how terrible for the
Earth and sea! For the devil has come down
To you, and he is filled with rage, because he
Knows that he has only a little time left."(12)

When the dragon realized that he had been thrown
Down to the earth, he began to purse the woman
Who had given birth to the boy.(13)

For Yahweh has given us dominion over him.
So put on the full armor of Yahweh so that you
Can stand against the devil's schemes. (Ephesians 6:11)
For we are not fighting against human beings
But against wicked spiritual forces in the heavenly
World, the rulers, authorities, and cosmic powers
Of this dark age. (Ephesians 6:12)

Therefore put on the full armor of God, so when
The day of evil comes, you may be able to stand
Your ground.

The adversary is seeking to devour whom he may,
And he knows that his time is short.
Do remember Isaiah 35:3-4
Strength the feeble hands, steady the knees
That give way; say to those with fearful hearts,
"Be strong, do not fear, your God will come,
He will come with vengeance; with divine
Retribution,
He will come to save you."

So be cure from this deadly disease of **Racism,
You-ism,** or other **Isms** that's been plague
In one self.
Passing it down to generation to generation.
Carrying on the adversary legacy.

Get rid of it!
And know that it's never about us.
It's the work of the beast.
But do remember what Yahweh
Has command.
Stand on His command and
His great commission.

Continue to remember Mathew 28:18
Then Yashua Jesus came to them and said,
"All authority in heaven and on earth
Has been given to Me."
Get to know Him, and the Nations
Will know that He is our
Resolution.

The Trumpets Growl

Weakness
ROMANS 1:28 Furthermore, since they did not think it worthwhile to retain the knowledge of God, he gave them over to depraved mind, to do what ought not to be done.

Weakness

What's your weakness?
Just to name a few.
If any applies to you.
Do a checklist
Then examine yourself in this plot:
Are your weakness
- Men
- Women
- Peer pressure
- Eating
- Gossiping
- Backbiting
- People pleasing
- Fornication
- Hatred
- Racism
- Slandering
- Cursing
- Disobedient
- Heartless
- Ruthless
- Senseless
- Faithless
- Lying
- Doubting
- Envy
- Boastful
- Flesh
- Stealing
- Greed
- Deceit
- Strife
- Murder
- Ignorance
- Betray
- Insolent

- Wickedness
- Witchcraft
- Depravity
- God haters
- Swearing
- Jealousy
- Misery
- Pride

Newsflash:
"Repent and turn away from it!"
Pray to GOD and ask for His help.
Seek the Kingdom of GOD
And His right standing.
Friend do it ! Before it's eternally too late.
Do invite Him in.
Jesus is standing at the door of your heart.
He is the **Only One** who can deliver you.
So friend let go and let GOD.

The Beginning, The End and Everything in Between

Revelation 21:6
And he said unto me, it is done. I am
Alpha and **Omega**, the beginning and
the end. I will give unto him that is
a thirst of the fountain of the water of
life freely.

Nehemiah 4:20
Wherever you hear the sound of the
Trumpet join us there. Our GOD will fight for us!

**The Beginning, The End
And Everything in Between**

IMAGES
GENESIS 6:5 The LORD saw that the wickedness of man was great
In the earth, and that every imagination of the thoughts of his heart was
Only evil continually.

GENESIS 6:6 And the LORD was sorry that He had made man on the
Earth, and it grieved Him to His heart.

Images

A gorgeous beautiful woman who was nine months pregnant.
She and her husband gave birth to a son and daughter.
The beautiful twins came into the world.
Yes! Proud parents they were.
The son who was so handsome.
The daughter so beautiful as she could be.

As the children grew up.
They had their own personality.
The parents had to work
To keep bread on the table;
And to keep up with their luxuries.

A trusted friend came over,
To watch the twins.
Mr. Disguise is what I will call him.
He sure won over the twins parents.
The son now who is around eight years old.
In his room watching videos.
Mr. Disguise knock on the door.
Then turn the doorknob.
"Can I come in? He did asked.
"Oh yes he do have manners!"
Sure said the innocent son.
Mr. Disguise did the unthinkable thing.
This will make you close your seeing eyes.
The son in shock can't believe,
What just happened?
But he didn't say anything.
Mr. Disguise said Shhhhhhhh!!!
We must not tell anyone.

That very next day.
Mr. Disguise repeated the same thing
To the daughter.
The daughter in shock , can't believe

What just happened?
But she didn't say anything.
Mr. Disguise said Shhhhhhh!!!
We must not tell anyone.
So the twins said nothing to each other.
They told no one , not even their parents.

Mr. Disguise came over everyday.
To keep an eye on the children.
While their parents are at work.

As the twins grew much older.
Their personality did change.
They went from cute, nice, handsome,
And beautiful.
To ugly , aggressive, confuse ,
And angry.
Their rolls did switch.
The son became the daughter.
And the daughter became the son.
It was an image that they betrayed.
The son said to himself.
"I am so confuse."
When I go outside all I see
Is Images.
The slogan that are on the billboards.
When I come home.
It's all on T.V.
When I go to the grocery store.
Images I see.
I picked up the magazines.
Images is what I see.
I went off to college.
Images all around me.
I saw some people just like me.
We introduce ourselves to each other.
We meet more friends.
As we recruited others.

They next thing I knew.
We formed an organization.
We have our own style of dressing.
We have our own clubs.
We have our own churches.
We have our own community.
Our friends were Lawyers, Doctors, Teachers,
Judges, Pastors, Bishops , and Politicians.
Our jobs were of high seated positions.
We party like there was no tomorrow.
But tomorrow has to come.
As the son knew within himself.
That was wrong;
Yet he felt that he couldn't escape.
Due to the powerful friends he knew.
So he gave his power to others.
So he could be with the in crowd.
He will himself to all types of spirits.
He made an image for himself.
Everyday he looked in the mirror.
But stirring back at him ,
Was his own image.
As he talked to himself.
I'll make myself look like this.
I'm going to wear that.
I'll bring so much attention to myself.
Everyone will want to be my friend.
I will continue to throw some wild parties.
I will supply the drugs and alcohol.
I will invite as many people that I can.
I will hire a D.J. .
I will have this party for two days.
My friends are going to love me,
Said the son.

The daughter said to herself.
I am so confuse.
When I go outside all I see

Is Images.
When I come home.
It's all on T.V.
When I go outside slogan are
On the billboards.
When I'm in the grocery store
Images I see.
"I picked up the magazines
Images is what I see!"
I went off to college.
Images all around me.
I saw some people,
Just like me.
We introduce ourselves to each other.
And began to hang around one another.
We meet more friends,
And we recruited others.
The next thing I knew.
We formed our own organization.
We have our own style of dressing.
We have our own clubs.
We have our own churches.
We have our own community.
Our friends were Nurses, Teachers, Doctors,
Lawyers, Judges, Bishops , Pastors, and Politicians.
Our jobs were of high seated positions.
We party like there was no tomorrow.
But tomorrow has to come.
As the daughter knew within herself,
That this is wrong.
Yet she felt like she couldn't escape.
Due to the powerful friends she knew.
So she gave her power to others.
She wanted to be with the in crowd.
Willing herself to all types of spirits.
She made an image for herself.
Everyday she looked in the mirror.
But stirring back at her ,

194

Was her own image.
As she talked to herself.
I'll make myself look like this.
I'm going to wear that.
I'll bring so much attention to myself.
Everyone will want to be my friend.
I will throw some wild parties.
I will supply the drugs and alcohol.
I will invite as many people as I can.
I will have the female strippers over.
I will hire a D.J..
I will have this party for two days.
I will tell them to invite,
People who are not like us.
When they see how we get down.
They will want to be like us.
"Said the daughter."
So she did what she intended to do.
After those two days of partying.
She felt a complete mess.
"But Yes!"
She kept up the charade.
As she talked to herself.
I was the life of that party.
I had everyone there.
I supplied everything.
I even recruited new friends.
"So", Why do I feel such a mess?
As she ran and yelled!
Lord , Why must this be?
Did I allow this to happened?
What is happening to me?
The tear came streaming down her face.
She dropped to her knees.
The Spirit from within spoke.
Why do you persecute Me?
She stopped and listen.
Why do you persecute Me?

The images you made were for yourself.
You made them become bigger than you.
You worship it.
You idolize it.
That's where you put all your attention.
I never left you.
You left Me.
Worship Me in Spirit and in Truth.
You love your idols.
More than you loved you.
I am a jealous God.
Put Me first before anyone.
That image you created,
Was self seeking.
It didn't come from Me.
You piled on those negative thoughts,
Until they became high.
That ritual you practice daily.
Seeking and searching for images,
And people who were like you.
Willing yourself to all kinds of
Ungodly foolishness.
You walked around,
Pretending that you were satisfied.
But when the lights goes out.
And you are alone.
A void you do feel.
You say to yourself.
This is the way I am.
God made me like this.
"But Oh No!"
When I spoke the earth into existence.
And made Creation in my image.
I saw that it was good.
That perpetrator won't escape.
Vengeance is mine.
But for those who created,
Their own image.

Didn't take on that of their Creator.
Remember Lucifer and a third of
His fallen angels.
They came down to the earth.
All they need were bodies.
As you allow those spirits to enter you.
You took on the accuser image.
For what happened to you from your pass.
The accuser disguise are,
Bitterness, envy, hatred, jealousy, liar,
thief, murder, covetous, two face deeds.
He come to kill , steal , and destroy.
He was an angel of light.
Then he became the angel of dark.
He has many disguises.
But you must not become his prey.
He entertain himself.
And you gave him a stage.
He recruits people.
And you were doing the ,
same thing too.
He tell them what they want to hear.
You did the same thing too.
He turned the truth into a lie.
And so did you.
He will show up anywhere.
You did that too.
He ran game on people.
And so did you.
He came to kill , steal and destroy.
You are doing that too.
He'll leave you in a world of confusion.
Now that's happening to you.
"Daughter," Now do this sound like your Maker?
Who created you.
I never left you.
You left Me.
You became your own god.

And took on the adversary image.
I had no choice.
But to turn away.
You were self seeking.
And allow the things to have you.
Repent and return to your God.
The One who formed and love you.
Turn from yourself, and your seeking ways.
Before it destroys you.
The enemy like to prey on your volubility.
That darkness that lies inside of you.
Vengeance is mine.
Allow me to take care of you.
Repent and turn from evil.
And I will abide in you.
The adversary know that his time is short.
And he want to take as many souls with him.
"I Am The LORD!"
Your soul belong to Me.
He may have violated you and took,
Your innocent.
This too he shall pay.
But you first must turn
From your wicked way.
Asked me to come in.
I AM at the door of your heart.
Waiting on you to invite Me in.
I never left you.
You left Me.
You worship those images.
That came from your mind.
You talk those images inside of you.
And that's what you became.
What you spoke into existence.
Then surrounded yourself around,
People that you thought,
Where like you.
Save yourself my child.

Put down those false idols.
Vengeance is mine.
And that enemy he will pay.
Repent, and I will put it in
The sea of forgetfulness.
Throw down your image.
Vengeance is mine.

The Lord went over to visit the son.
He was wrestling with himself.
The partying is over.
His friends , they all wore disguises.
He thought about,
Mr. Disguise.
He grew angry , throwing the furniture around.
"I hate you!"
You told me not to tell.
My parents know none of this.
Mr. Disguise you are from hell.
Now I am left in a world of confusion.
The son burst out with a yell!!
Lord Why must this be?
Did I allow this to happened?
As the tears rolled down his face.
He dropped to his knees.
The Spirit from within spoke.
Why do you persecute Me?
The image you made was for yourself.
You made them become bigger that you.
You worship it.
That's where you put all of your attention.
I never left you.
You left Me.
Those who love Me
Worship Me in Spirit and in Truth.
You loved your idols.
More than you love you.
I Am a jealous God.

Put Me first before anyone.
That image you created,
Was self seeking.
It didn't come from Me.
You piled on those negative thoughts,
Until they became so high.
That ritual you practice daily.
Seeking and searching for images,
And other people who were like you.
Willing yourself to all kinds ,
Of ungodly foolishness.
You walked around pretending,
That you were satisfied.
But when the lights goes out,
And you are alone.
A void you do feel.
You say to yourself.
This is the way that I am.
God made me like this.
"But Oh No!"
When I spoke the universe into existence,
And made Creation in My Image.
I saw that it was good.
That perpetrator won't escape.
Vengeance is mine!
But for those who created their own image.
Didn't take on the form of their Creator.
Remember Lucifer and a third of his angels.
Who fell from heaven.
They came down to the earth.
All they needed were bodies.
As you allow those spirits to enter you.
You took on the accuser image.
From your past.
The son yelled!
"No you allow this to happened.
I was just a child.
My son, the Kingdom belong

To little children as such as you.
I will avenge.
Your sin I will remember no more.
I will put it in the sea of forgetfulness.
But you must repent, and turn towards Me.
So the son yelled!
"Lord I didn't cause this to be."
Mr. Disguise came and
He violated me!
Son , I'll explain it to you this way.
Your parents had Mr. Disguise
As their trusted friend.
Mr. Disguise won your parents trust.
He said all the right things.
He did all the right stuff.
He showered you and your sister
With beautiful gifts.
He brought you, toys, video games.
And a puppy.
He brought designer clothes.
He brought you expensive shoes.
He put money in your pocket.
He took you and your sister to school.
He told your parents,
Don't come home.
Stay at work late if you have too.
I will take care of the children.
I will make sure their homework is done.
I will feed them.
And I will make sure they
Want for nothing.
Those were his words.
So your parents put all their trust
Into their friend.
And so did you and your sister.
You all knew him.
He came around everyday.
See Mr. Disguise knew just,

When to go on his prey.
He pacified you with ,
So many beautiful gifts.
Then he took your innocent away
On that awful day.
I did sounded the alarm.
You see Mr. Disguise,
Was already in your parents ear.
He went on your parents jobs.
He loaded them down ,
With so much work.
He whispered in their Bosses ear.
You have a deadline to meet.
Offer your employees some overtime.
So you could get this work out.
Mr. Disguise was running to and fro.
He never gives up.
He never goes to sleep.
He is the angel of darkness.
He has his own employees,
They work with him.
While they have taken on the adversary,
Assignment ,and his spirit.
Grabbing as many as they can.
They enter one's mind.
If you are not paying attention.
While your parents were loaded down
With all of their work on their job.
They lost focus.
They gave their authority to someone else.
Mr. Disguise , As we like to call him.
He had his game already in motion.
His fallen angels gave him the head up.
That's when he attacked you.
On that awful dreaded day.
What he did.
Yes is so wrong.
Son don't blame Me.

I did sounded the alarm.
Not just one time.
But as often as I could.
Your parents were satisfied.
With the big fancy house.
Four car garage.
The plasma televisions.
The designer clothes.
Their prestige friends.
Their brand name cars,
And what people thought of them.
Now after working over time
From their jobs.
You the children were all tuck in.
They could only give you a kiss
 On the forehead.
And repeated the same thing
The very next day.
While Mr. Disguise and his
Disciple search for the next house.
They look for homes that has no order.
And the again,
Mr. Disguise he is so tricky.
He will look for homes that are in order.
They both are equal.
One can not talk about the other.
He becomes everyone's prey.
It doesn't matter, rather rich or poor.
Mr. Disguise is waiting
At someone's door.
If you don't open it
He will try another way.
Don't blame Me
I sounded the alarm.
The tears rolled down the son face.
"So now you are saying
That it's my parents fault.?"
My son everyone has a

Still small voice within.
A person my say to themselves.
I should have done this.
But yet I choose to do that.
Why didn't I pay attention.
I heard the alarm sounding softly.
No! No! No! No!,
But your thoughts was screaming,
Yes! Yes! Yes! Yes!.
Then you choose.
Now Mr. Disguise has you in a mess.
He enters the mind.
He will pump you up.
And tell you everything,
That you want to hear.
No, My son I'm not saying,
That it's your parents fault.
They are so bless.
With two beautiful children.
They are bless with this fancy home,
The cars, and that
High paying job position,
That I bless them with.
Somehow they allow the stuff ,
To have them.
As they reach out for more and more.
Their tongue became boastful.
They became lovers of themselves.
I sounded the alarm.
But their images grew.
Bigger and bigger , and bigger.
So the son began to understand.
He wiped his eyes.
"I blame you LORD for everything."
The son said.
And the LORD said, "I know, I know.
They all do.
But you must not forget about Lucifer.

The one who masquerade around
Town , seeking to devour whomever he can.
I will avenge.
You are my instrument.
 But I can't come in.
And why can't you asked the son?
I am having a talk with you now.
Just as Mr. Disguise stood at door.

Let Me explain the difference.
I stand at the door of your heart.
Mr. Disguise stand at the door
Of your head.
I love my children.
He hates his children.
I came to give them life abundance.
He came to destroy.
I came to give eternal life.
He came to bring eternal death.
I came to deliver you from bondage.
He came to capture.
I came to set the captive free.
He came to steal as many as he can.
I came as Truth.
He came as a liar.
The son was beginning to understand.
So why did you continue to ,
Allow this to happened?
Son as you grew older.
You and your sister, thought that
It was the right thing to do.
You both had so much stuff,
That pacified you.
No where in your life.
You had Me.
It wasn't My Spirit that had you.
Mr. Disguise had the both of you
At such a young age.

I will avenge!
He know that his time is short.
He is going to pay.
"I Am the LORD."
The son asked.
What am I suppose to do?
Repent and turn from your sinful ways.
I will avenge.
The adversary will pay.
The son did as the Lord
Directed him to do.
With out stretched arms the son.
Surrender, Lord I surrender all to You!
I became this image.
Something that I planted in my head.
As I walked around in darkness.
Wishing that I was dead.
Mr. Disguise took so many.
He even had me.
I was running around to and fro.
Using my own body.
Grabbing as many that I could.
I learned this from my teacher.
Showering the innocent with,
Beautiful gifts.
I supplied everything,
Telling them what they wanted to hear.
This image that I created.
I made it bigger than myself.
I called myself a diva.
I masquerade in many costumes.
I will myself to Mr. Adversary.
I became his prey.
He shut my seeing eyes.
As the darkness enter me.
There was no light.
Knowing full well that I couldn't see.
I kept up this charade.

206

Knowing that it wasn't okay.
But I had the people, the friends,
The job and the money.
Not realizing that the stuff had me.
I'm willing to turn from the evil.
That had me bound.
Mr. Disguise had me in his trap.
I was in a web.
No one told me that there was,
An escape plan.
The organization that I choose.
It has the same people in it.
They were people like me.
This looked normal to me.
"So I thought."
This is the way it suppose to be.
I felt deep, deep, down inside
Of me, that this may be wrong.
But I had the friends ,that cheered
Me on.
Somehow my conscience would
Continue to speak.
After I have done the wrong.
Then I would say to myself,
Something is wrong.
Something different is going on.
But no, I would talk myself out of it.
I wanted to please everybody.
And not myself.
I became what everyone , wanted
Me to be.
"I Am her my son said the LORD."
Do have reverence for Me.
Your sin I will remember no more.
I will avenge.
Put down your false image.
I will avenge.
Give every situation and ,

Circumstance over to me.
I Am The Lord.
The only one who can make you free.
Remember what I said.
Repent and turn to Me.
I Am The LORD.
I will avenge!
Put down your false idols.
And turned towards Me.
I Am The LORD .
I will avenge.
That Serpent , Lucifer, Accuser,
Satan, Mr. Disguise.
He will pay for the lies, and
Destruction he did on that
Dreaded awful day.

The Beginning, The End
And Everything in Between

It's A New Year
ECCLESIASTES 3:12-15 So I realized that all we can do is be happy
And do the best we can while we are still alive.

All of us should eat drink and enjoy what we have worked for. It is
God's gift.

I know that everything God does will last forever. You can't add
Anything from it or take anything away from it. And one thing God
Does is to make us stand in awe of Him.

Whatever happens or can happen has already happened before. God
Makes the same thing happen again and again.

It's A New Year

At the dawn of a New Year
What do you do?
Do you make resolution
To stop this or that?
Do thus and so?
Go here and there?

At the dawn of a New Year
Are you out and about?
At a club?
A party?
A New Year's celebration?

At the dawn of a New Year
Are you dancing to loud beats?
Banging on loud drums?
Throwing confetti and twirling sparkles?

At the dawn of a New Year
People usually gather in large numbers
Reminiscing of times past
Hopeful of times to come
Dancing, singing, drinking, shouting.

When my New Year comes in
I will thank Yah
For another year
Of health
Soundness of mind
Family safety.
Love of friends.

Like a butterfly
Transformed from the cocoon.
A New Year is a new beginning.
At the dawn of a New Year
Old things are passed away.

The Beginning, The End
And Everything in Between

Take It Away
PSALMS 88:1-2 LORD God, my Savior, I cry out all day, and night
I come before you.

Hear my prayer; listen to my cry for help!

Take It Away

Take it away, Yah.
Anything that's not of You.

Take it away. Yah.
Anything you see
That's not fit for me.

Take it away, Yah
And give me the things
You want me to have.

Fill me, Yah
With the fullness of You.
Fill me, Yah
With you precious Spirit.

Let Your Spirit teach me
To do the things that are of You.

Let Your Spirit show me
And guide me on what to do.

And when I do the things
That are from You,
Let my Spirit continue
To bless Yashua, who abides
In all the things I do.

The Beginning, The End
And Everything in Between

Chasing After the Wind
ECCLESIASTES 2:11 Then I thought about all that I had done and how
Hard I had worked doing it, and I realized that it didn't mean a thing. It
Was like chasing the wind of no use at all.

Chasing After the Wind

Wanted a cool, sweet breeze,
So I chased the wind
But I didn't catch it.

Wanted a cool, sweet breeze
So I attained houses and land.
I invested in stocks and bonds.
I earned college degrees.
Not just one, but three.
My children ask for nothing
And receive it all.

That's my cool, sweet breeze.
But I settled for less.
No one told me
At the end of my life
All I had would profit me nothing.
Nothing eternal.

Fear of upsetting me
Preventing them from telling me
I was being my own god.
Chasing my own cool, sweet breeze.

Fear they wouldn't get their portion
Of the lions share
Kept them from saying to me,
'Just stand still.
You'll feel
The cool, sweet breeze
All over you.

The Beginning, The End
And Everything in Between

A Seed Of Truth
MATHEW 28: 19-20 Go, then, to all peoples everywhere and make them
My disciples: baptize them in the name of the Father, the Son, and the
Holy Spirit,

And teach them to obey everything I have commanded you. And I will
Be with you always, to the end of the age.

A Seed Of Truth

On my way to work yesterday
I planted a seed.

Clear, crisp fall Monday
Wind singing a whispering, chilly song
Tree branches dancing
Leaves dusting the city pavement.
A man, appearing 42, but maybe much younger
Walked up beside me
He wore layers of torn, old clothing
Tattered long winter coat
Gloves torn, cracked, weathered fingers exposed
A deep, tired, scratchy voice
Said to me, "Spare change for something to eat?"

I looked at the man, just for a moment
Eyes empty, hands trembling
Knowing at once
His was a life hard
Not unlike my own-years past.
A kind soul planted a seed for me one day.
He could have so easily left me there.

Instantly, the man became my teacher
Heaven gave me a chance
To plant
A seed of truth
On fertile ground
So I said to the man,
"All the change in my pocket
Couldn't buy enough for your hunger."

I know you
I am you
Spirits you seek won't satisfy your hunger.

I know
I am you.

The seed of the Spirit
Multiplies 1000 times
5 fish and 2 loaves of bread

Take this seed that grows from my mouth
To your waiting heart
I know you wait
I am you and you are me

A brief respite
Is all you get
From that which you seek
Nothing to calm the nagging hunger
Raging in your soul.

I know you
I am you
All you want is to be fed
A feast that silver coins
Cannot buy
It's free
This is the seed of truth:
You will not be satisfied
Until you find
Within
The Spirit
Fills your cup
Runs over

Love feeds your Spirit
You hunger no more

Take this seed that grows from my mouth
To your waiting heart

Talk within
Not without
You will find within
That Spirit

He watched my eyes intently
Searching for truth there
The yearning in his eyes
Affirmed me as his student

Heaven gave me a chance
To plant a seed
On fertile ground
My teacher said to me,
"God Bless You"
With that
Turned and walked away

He blessed me
Heaven gave me a chance
To plant a seed
On fertile ground
The seed had been planted.

The Beginning, The End
And Everything in Between

We All Grieve

Luke 9:6
So with you, now is the time of
Grief, but I will see you again
And you will rejoice and no one
Will take away your joy.

We All Grieve

I grieve.
You grieve.
Grief is appropriate.
At the premature loss of innocence
Premature death of a loved one.
Grief is appropriate.

Accidents happen everyday.
Death is past of this existence.
A passing from the state
To another.
We all grieve together.

The loss of friends and family
To a world of death and darkness
Brings bitter grief
To those who've glimpsed The Light.

Let grief take its natural course.
But in this state
Tarry not, unnecessarily.
The Father is yet in need
Of workers in His vineyard.

The Beginning, The End
And Everything in Between

Love

GALATIANS 5: 22-23 But the Spirit produces love, joy, peace, patience,
Kindness, goodness, faithfulness,

Humility, and self control. There is no law against such things as these.

EPHESIANS 4:15-16 Instead, by speaking the truth in a spirit of love
We must grow up in every way to Christ, who is the head.

Under His control all the different parts of the body fit together, and
The whole body is held together by every joint with which it is provided.
So when each separate part words as it should, the whole body grows and
Builds itself up through love.

JOHN 15:12 My commandment is this : love one another, just as I love you.

1JOHN 3:11 The message you heard from the very beginning is this we
Must love one another.

1JOHN 3:12 We must not be like Cain; he belonged to the Evil One and
Murdered his own brother Abel. Why did Cain murder him?
Because the things he himself did were wrong, and things his brother
Did was right.

1JOHN 4:7 Dear friends, let us love one another, because love comes from
God. Whoever loves is a child of God and knows God.

1JOHN 4:8 Whoever does not love does not know God, for God is love.

1JOHN 4:9 And God showed His love for us by sending His only Son
In the world, so that we might have life through Him.

1JOHN 4:10 This is what love is: it is not that we have loved God, but
That He loved us and sent His Son to be the means by which our sins
Are forgiven.

1JOHN 4:11 Dear friends, if this is how God loved us, then we should
Love one another.

1JOHN 4:16 And we ourselves know and believe the love which God has
For us. God love, and whoever lives in love lives in union with God and
God lives in union with him.

1JOHN 4:19 We love because God first loved us.

1JOHN 4:21 The command the Christ has given us is this: whoever loves
God must love his brother also.

Love

Love is living.
Love is sharing.
Love is caring.
Love is compassionate.
Love is giving
Love is forgiving.
Love is hope.
Love is faith.
Love is kind.
Love is patience.
Love is peaceful.
Love is joyful.
Love is understanding.
Love is tolerant.
Love is enduring.
Love is humility.

If I have none of these
I don't have love.

The Beginning, The End
And Everything in Between

He's Not a Genie
PROVERB 17:20 A man of perverse heart does not prosper; he who tongue is deceitful fall into trouble

He's Not a Genie

He's not a Genie;
One you pick up at will,
Rub to gratify your wishes,
Lay again on the shelf.
To be used another day
Another way.

The bottle, you see,
Has a principle of three:
The number of wishes
On demand.
Those three
One can only receive.
Now you and I know
If three is all you get,
There is no way
That He
Is a Genie.

But we treat Him as such
Like our command is His wish.
As if
The creature can wield
The Creator.
Not so.
What have we to do
With the sun, stars, moon.
Everest's greatest peak
Or the high wind's dune?

Yet we think
I'll call upon Him
When I need Him…
And He'll be there
Rescuing me from folly.
Or danger

Or financial woes
Or grief
Or pain
Or anything I wish.
That is His use.
That is my wish.

His mercy is great
On our foolish hearts
That recognize not
He's not a Genie.

The Beginning, The End
And Everything in Between

I Surrender
PSALM 86:3 You are my God, so be merciful to me;

PSALM 86:10 You are mighty and do wonderful things;
You alone are God.

PSALM 86:11 Teach me, LORD, what you want me to do,
And I will obey You faithfully; Teach me to serve you with
Complete devotion.

I Surrender

Can't think right
Can't see right
Can't talk right
Can't act right
May as well give up.

The greatest wisdom:
To recognize
I
Am
Nothing.

The greatest work:
I
Am
Ignorant

The greatest act:
Surrender

The Beginning, The End
And Everything in Between

Riding In My Car
JOB 28:24 Because He sees the end of the earth, sees everything under
The sky.

Riding In My Car

One day I was riding in my car.
Road rage everywhere.
The blue car
Cut in front of the red car.

The Beamer didn't stop
For the Lexus.
The Mercedes had the right-of –way.
The Volvo didn't yield in the merge lane.

I said to myself
There are people in those cars
And spirits in those people.
Do they know
That as they drive
Those top name brand cars
That everything we know
Could simply cease to be?

While Ms. Volvo
Gives the finger to Mr. Mercedes,
And Granny Lexus
Frowns at Beamer Jr.,
Yahweh is nearing the end of the script
No more road rage
No more road.

I said to myself
As I was riding in my car.
And then I asked myself
Are you ready for this to be over
Lick-a-Dee split?

I asked this of myself
As I was riding in my car.

The Beginning, The End
And Everything in Between

Heavenly
GENESIS 2:2 By the seventh day God finished what He had
Been doing and stopped working.

GENESIS 2:3 He blessed the seventh day and set it apart as a
Special day, because by that day He had completed His creation
And stopped working.

EXODUS 20:8 Observe the Sabbath and keep it holy.

EXODUS 20:9 You have six days in which to do your work,

EXODUS 20:10 But the seventh day is a day of rest dedicated to Me.

EXODUS 20:11 In the six days I , the LORD made the earth, the sky
The seas, and everything in them, but on the seventh day I rested.
That is why I , the LORD blessed the Sabbath and made it holy.

Heavenly

You have made all things possible
    within Yourself.
Your choice gifts of,
Faith
Wisdom
Knowledge
Love
Understanding

It has given me the strength,
To move on
To go on
To live on
And to listen to Your Spirit that lies
    within.

Your heavenly dwelling is a place of
    rest.
There I found that rest.
And with You, I have seen the good,
I have seen the bad;
But all the things that I have seen.
The good out weighed the bad.

So within You,
And through You,
I will rest.

For all good and perfect gifts come
    from You,
When others decide to rest in You, they
    will have.
Faith
Joy
Hope
Peace

Love
Wisdom
Knowledge
Understanding
Patience
Faithfulness
Self-Control
Kindness
Gentleness
Meekness
Forgiveness

And from all those special gifts,
That are of goodness,
We should be able to
Transfer those gifts,
And allow our light to shine
Towards others.
So they may see
The fruit of the spirit.
And from their they
Could be at rest.

The Beginning, The End
And Everything in Between

Touch The Hem Of His Garment
MATHEW 9:21 She said to herself,
"If I only touch His cloak, I will be healed."

Touch The Hem Of His Garment

She said to herself,
"If I only touch His cloak, I will be healed."

Again!

She said to herself,
"If I only touch His Cloak, I will be healed."

Again!

She said to herself,
"If I only touch His cloak, I will be healed."

Again!

She said to herself
"If I only touch His cloak, I will be healed."

Again!

She said to herself
"If I only touch His cloak, I will be healed."

Again!

She said to herself
"If I only touch His cloak, I will be healed."

Again!

She said to herself
"If I only touch His cloak, I will be healed."

Weaken and walking with blur vision.
Not knowing what was wrong with her.

Yet still pressing her way on.
And saying to herself.
"If I only touch His cloak, I will be healed."

She's trying, she's trying,
Digging deeper and deeper
And deep within her spirit.

She's getting closer and closer
But though it seem so far.
She kept reaching and reaching.
For it seem like something want
To pull her away.

Again!

She kept repeating to herself.
"If I only touch His cloak, I will be healed."
Her faith began to rise.

She get stronger and stronger.
She applied that scripture to her life.
As she reached and touch that cloak.
She was made whole.

**The Beginning, The End
And Everything in Between**

The Flesh
ROMANS 8:15 For the spirit that God has given you does not make you
Slaves and cause you to be afraid; instead, the spirit makes you God's
Children, and by the spirit's power we cry out to God,
"Father my Father!"

The Flesh

Empty
Desire…
    Wanting to escape
      The emptiness
        Finding relief…
……………oh, yes
That's better
Time passes
Reflection comes
Desire to escape
The wanting to
Find relief
Oh, yes
That's better
Reflection comes
The circle continues.

"O wretched man that I am!
Who shall deliver me
From the body of this death?"

"I thank Yashua through the Messiah
So then, with the mind I myself
Serve the law of Elohim
But with the flesh the law of sin."

"There is therefore now
No condemnation to them
Which are in Yashua the Messiah,
Who walk not after the flesh
But after the Spirit."

Know this and be free from
The flesh.

The Beginning, The End
And Everything in Between

Lift Me
PSALM 24:6 Such is the generation of those who seek Him.
Who seek your face, O God of Jacob.

PSALM 24:7 Lift up your heads, O you gates; be lifted up,
You ancient doors, that The King Of Glory may come in.

Lift Me

Lift me higher and higher and higher.
LORD help me to walk this mile.

I had everything
I had a diamond in the palm of my hand.
I had the big cars, houses, and a fine job.
I had just about everything.

But One Person I did not have
And that was Jesus.
He was the One Who has provided everything for me.
LORD help me to walk one mile.

I know that You will walk with me.
Let Your words guide me into the light.

Lift me higher and higher and higher.
Lord I need You every hour.
You came to rescue me time after time,
But still I failed.

I can do nothing without You.
The moment came when
I had lost my strength.
Yet I did remember what my parent
Deposit inside of me.
But I didn't use those words
Until I was at my last end.
My parent taught me about
The power of prayer
And all about You.

But yet I allow my ego
To get in the way.
For I was feeling ashamed
And unworthy to call on Your name.

Then the walls were closing in on me.
Still I can remember from a child
What was deposit inside of me.
Then to You I cried out.

LORD, lift me higher and higher and higher
I need You every hour.
Come and rest inside of me
Help me to reach that place
Where I need to be.

Lord I can't do this alone.
I have tried
And it left me in a mess.
Please don't turn Your face away from me.
Help me to reach that place
Where I need to be.

Lift me higher and higher and higher.
LORD do restore me.
Bring me to the place
Where You see is best for me.

The Beginning The End
and Everything In Between

BLOOD
JOHN 6:53 Then Jesus said unto them, verily , I say to you, except ye eat
The flesh of the Son of Man, and drink His blood, ye have no life in you.

JOHN 6:54 Whoso eat my flesh, and drink my blood, hath eternal life, and
I will raise him up at the last day.

JOHN 6:55 For My flesh is meat indeed, and my blood is drink indeed.

JOHN 6:56 He that eat my flesh and drink my blood, dwell in Me, and
I in him.

BLOOD

Power in the blood
We sing the song in our Tabernacles
But did we really hear the words?
Look, meditate on these words.
"Power in the Blood"
Stop!
What are your thoughts?
Did you feel anything?
Let me take you back to where it began.
Remember when Cain killed his brother Abel
This is what God said to Cain.
Where is your brother Abel?
"Cain said, I don't know, am I my brother's keeper.
Second lie,
First murder.
But there is power in the blood
You see Cain thought that no one was watching
Though he may have thought the area was secluded
And no one was watching.
But God was!
You see Abel blood cried out
To God from the ground
There is power in the blood.
"So much power"
You see when someone is being murder
In the streets or in their homes.
The blood is so powerful
That it does leave stains.
You tried to remove it
But it won't wash away.
Oh the memories will not erase.
The trail and traces are still there
So you put yourself under a curse.
Once the blood that was shed touches
The ground,
The ground open up it's mouth

To receive that blood.
The blood had a voice.
You see the blood cried out.
God saw,
He heard
Now the curse has fallen on you.
Your conscience has you.
You wrestle with your self.
Wondering if anyone saw
Or know what you just did.
Walking on the face of the earth
Remembering and seeing the blood
That was all over your hands.
There is power
Power in the Blood
It has a voice.
The voice cried out
God saw,
He knows,
And He heard
How powerful is the blood
Think about what to do.
Before you do the do.
If blood is shed
Your conscience will bother you
If any man touches you.
That person will suffer vengeance
Seven times over.
This is what the LORD did
He put a mark on Cain
So that no one would kill him.
But if any man does,
He will suffer vengeance
Seventy seven times before
The first murder.
The circle continue
The blood has a voice.
The ground open up it's mouth

To receive the blood
The blood cried out.

God saw,
He knows,
He heard
Your conscience will bother you.
If any man touches you,
He will suffer vengeance
Seventy hundred seventy seven times
The circle continues.
Power in the Blood.

Stop!
Meditate
What are your thoughts?
I know you are thinking now!

Newsflash: The blood in the body brings life.
Once the blood leaves the body, there is no life.
Choose life not death or murder.
Free your mind, give it to the Lord.

Think about what you do.
Before you do the do.
Circles, they do go around and around.
"The blood, it too has a voice."
And there is **Power in the Blood**.

The Beginning, the End
and Everything in Between

Piercing
PSALM 22:7 All who see Me mock Me; they hurl insults, shaking their heads.

PSALM 22:14 I Am poured out like water and all my bones are out of joint, My heart has melted away within Me.

PSALM 22:16 Dogs have surrounded Me; a band of evil men encircled Me, They have pierced My hands and feet.

Piercing

What is piercing?
Where is your piercing?
Is it on the ear?
Is it on the nose?
Is it on the tongue?
Is it on the navel?
What does your piercing represent?
Was it for fashion?
Was it a dare?
Think about it!
Was your piercing done, because
Everyone else were doing it?
Think about it!

Well, I have a story about
This Man's piercing.
He was bound.
They took a sharp instrument
Which had hooks with pieces
As He leaned forward
Their hands went up
With that braided leather strap
As it went across His back.
"Slash!"
His skin came opened
They lash Him again
The hooks with sharp pieces
 Embedded itself through the skin.
Cutting Him again
Causing deep contusions
"Slash!"
As His skin
Slit open again!
That braided whip

Cut into the skin and

subcutaneous tissue
"Slash!"
They whipped Him again!
Screams of blood
Came running down
From out of His skin.
"Slash!"
They whipped Him
Again and again.
Repeating the same
Thing over again.
The laceration tore
Into His skeletal muscle
Yashua Jesus cried
From within.
As those hooks did much
Damage to His lovely skin.

His piercing wasn't over
They twisted a crown of thorns,
And put it on His head.
They stripped Him;

Then they dressed Him in a purple robe.
They put a staff in His right hand,
Then knelt down in front
And mocked Him.

They struck Him in the head with a staff,
Over and over again.
As He offered His cheeks
They pulled out the hair from His beard.
Then they spit in His face.
And struck Him with their fists.
Mocking Him; while others
Slapped Him, and said
"Prophesy to us Christ
Who hit you?"

When brought to the chief priest
And his officials, they shouted
Crucify Him!
Crucify Him!

After that, they took off His robe
And put His own clothes on Him.

Then they made a bet
To decide who will get His clothes;
Yes, that's what they did!

They even force Him to carry
His own cross.
Then they took Him to a place
Called Golgotha.
Right here is where they Crucify Him!
As the nail pierced through the left wrist.
Which is part of His hand.
"Bump!, Bump!, Bump!"
Streams of blood came running down.
As the nail pierced through the right wrist.
Which is part of His hand.
"Bump!, Bump!, Bump!"
Streams of blood came running down.
They repeated the same thing.
This time to His feet.
As the nail pierced through His feet.
"Bump!, Bump!, Bump!"
Streams of blood came running down
From the flesh and ligaments.
As He stayed up there.
Took His piercing like a Man.
He said nothing.
He did nothing.
Innocent was this Man.
While He was hung high and

Stretched wide.
The people stood around
Like they were watching a show.
He gave His all to them.
They betrayed Him.
He had their backs.
But no one had His.
He gave.
We took.
He lost.
We gained.

Yes, they place a notice above His head.
Written in three languages .
This is what it read:

This Jesus, The King of the Jews.
Here's another notice that read:
Let this Christ, this King of Israel.

Here's another notice that read:
Jesus of Nazareth The King of the Jews.
Here's another notice that read:
This is The King of the Jews.
Which can be read it in Latin, Greek and Aramaic.

As they stood their watching
And even sneered at Him.
They said" He saved others, let Him save
Himself if He is the Messiah of God
The Chosen One.

As He stayed up there
Nailed to the cross
Mathew one of Jesus disciple wrote this:
He spoke these words
"Eloi, Eloi, lama sabach-thani?
"My God, My God, Why have You forsaken Me?"

Luke, another of Jesus disciple wrote this:
"Father, forgive them, for they do not know
What they are doing.

John, another of Jesus disciple wrote this:
"I Am Thirsty."
As His tongue sticks to the roof of His mouth;
They soaked a sponge that had wine vinegar
On it and lifted it to the Messiah.
Then He said
"It Is Finish."

With that He bowed His head
And gave up His Spirit.
Then one of the soldiers pierced Yashua Jesus
On the side with his spear.
Flows of blood and water came out.
Not one of His bone were broken.

For the people will look on the **One**
They have pierced.
With all of that," which were said and told
Now tell Him, have your piercing
Have such meaning as that?

The Beginning, The End
And Everything in Between

The Cross

ISAIAH 53:2 He grew up before Him like a tender shoot, and like
A root out of dry ground. He had no beauty or majesty to attract us
To Him, nothing in His appearance that we should desire Him.

ISAIAH 53:5 But He was pierced for our transgressions, He was
Crushed for our iniquities; the punishment that brought us peace
Was upon Him, and by His wounds we are healed.

ISAIAH 53:6 We all, like sheep, have gone astray, each of us has
Turned to his own way; and the LORD has on Him the iniquity of
Us all.

ISAIAH 53:7 He was oppressed and afflicted, yet He did not open
His mouth; He was led like a lamb to the slaughter, and as a sheep
Before her shearers is silent, so He did not open His mouth.

ISAIAH 53:8 By oppression and judgment He was taken away. And
Who can speak of His descendants? For He was cut off from the
Land of the living; for the transgression of my people He was stricken.

ISAIAH 53:9 He was assigned a grave with the wicked, and with the
Rich in His death, though He had done no violence; nor was any deceit
In His mouth.

PSALM 22:1-2 My God, my God, why have you abandoned Me?
I have cried desperately for help, but still it does not come.

During the day I call to You, my God but You did not answer; I call
At night but get no rest.

The Cross

When I'm too high and mighty
Belligerent, crass and feisty
Eventually
I remember the cross.

When I'm down on my fate
And think there's too much on my plate
Eventually
I remember the cross.

When my mind's not at ease
I'm the one I aim to please
Eventually
I remember the cross.

At this crucial moment in time
He died
To be the perfect sacrifice
Foretold in testaments past.
Sacrifice for sins
Too many to number
All evil
Warranting death:
Vanity and pride
The greatest deceivers
Every time.
Once recognized,
I remember
The cross
Where the Savior
Died
Then was Buried
And **rose again**
It's never about me
It's all about Him.
And what He was

On
The Cross

255

The Beginning, The End
And Everything in Between

I Have Risen
MATHEW 28:6 He is not here; He has risen, just as He said.
Come and see the place where He lay.

I Have Risen

Do not stand and my grave and weep.
I Am not there
I have risen.
I Am in the wind
That gently blows.
I Am in the snow.
I Am in the flowers that bloom.
I Am with you at dusk, noon and evening.
I Am in the Sun that set and beam.
I Am in the moon.
I Am with you where ever you go.
I Am in the stars that sparkles at night.
I Am hidden in clouds that sit in the sky.
I Am in the Universe.
I Am the Truth and the Light.
I Am in the hearts of all my children.
I came to fulfill.
It had to be done.
I was talk about in testaments told.
Do not stand at my grave and weep;
I Am not there
I Have Risen.

The Beginning, The End
And Everything in Between

Haven't You Heard
MATHEW 9:12-13 Yashua / Jesus heard them and answered,
"People who are well do not need a doctor, but only those
Who are sick.

Go and find out what is meant by the scripture that says:
'It is kindness that I want, not animal sacrifice. I have not
Come to call respectable people, but outcasts.

Haven't You Heard

Mr. and Mrs. High Mighty, who are so sadist.
They didn't show pity on anyone.
This couple goes around with their noses in the air.
Who gave no concern or care.
They walked pass the unfortunate, look and stir.
Next they make all sorts of comments, about;
Why are they sitting there?

"Mr. Mighty said, Lord I am glad that's not me."
Look at us, we are Mr. and Mrs. High Mighty.
They sit, stand, and walk with signs around their necks.
Look! Mr. Mighty, pointed Mrs. Mighty.
They look like they want to come over here with us!
Mr. Mighty said, hey the better not!
For I will point them in the direction to the nearest bus.
"Where will they get the money ?
I don't know Mr. Mighty said,
I don't care just get away from us.

I know honey they look so filthy and unclean.
We don't want those spirits rubbing off on us.
We are Mr. and Mrs. High Mighty
Haven't you heard.
We're better than they are,
And we go to church every Sunday
To get our praise on.

Look over there
More beggars
Walking up and down
In front of the church.
Why don't they just go
Inside and hear the word?

"Come on honey!
Pay no attention to them."

We must go inside
To hear the man
Of God speak the word.

Why don't we sit over there
With the other Pastors and Deacons?
They are the best seats in the building.

"Here comes **The Angel of The Lord**!"
He is ready to give the church
The **Word** for today.
The Angel of The Lord
Begin to speak.
Will you open up your **Bibles** to
MATHEW 9:12-13
Then Mr. and Mrs. High Mighty
Sank down in their seats
Looking like
Mr. and Mrs. Convicted.

The Beginning, The End
And Everything in Between

What I Like About Christmas

LUKE 1:5 In the time of Herod king of Judas was a priest named
Zechariah, who belonged to the priestly division of Abijah; his wife
Elizabeth was also a descendent of Aaron.

LUKE 1:6 Both of them were upright in the sight of God, observing
All the Lord's commandments and regulations blamelessly.

LUKE 1:7 But they had no children, because Elizabeth was barren.

LUKE 1:13 But the angel said to him: "Do not be afraid, Zechariah;
Your prayer has been heard; Your wife Elizabeth will bear you a son
And you are to give him the name John.

LUKE 1:14 He will be a joy and delight to you, and many will rejoice
Because of his birth,

LUKE 1:15 For he will be great in the sight of the Lord. He is never
To take wine or other fermented drink, and he will he filled with the
Holy Spirit even from birth.

*LUKE 1:24 After this his wife Elizabeth became pregnant and for
Five months remained in seclusion.

*LUKE 1:26 In the sixth month, God sent the angel Gabriel to
Nazareth, a town in Galilee,

LUKE 1:27 To a virgin pledge to be married to a man named Joseph,
A descendant of David. The virgin name was Mary.

LUKE 1:28 The angel went to her and said," Greeting, you are highly
Favored! The Lord is with you."

*LUKE 1:31 You will be with child and give birth to a son, and
You are to give him the name Yashua /Jesus.

262

LUKE 1:32 He will be great and will be called the Son of the Most High. The Lord God will give him the throne of His father David,

LUKE 1:33 And He will reign over the house of Jacob forever: His Kingdom will never end.

LUKE 1:34 "How will this be, "Mary asked the angel," since I am A virgin?"

LUKE 1:35 The angel answered, "The Holy Spirit will come upon You , and the power of the Holy One to be born will be called The Son of God.

*LUKE 1:36 Even Elizabeth your relative is going to have a child In her old age, and she who was said to be barren is in her sixth month.

LUKE 1:39 At that time Mary got ready and hurried to town in the Hill country of Judea,

LUKE 1:40 Where she entered Zechariah's home and greeted Elizabeth.

LUKE 1:41 When Elizabeth heard Mary's greeting, the baby leaped In her womb, and Elizabeth was filled with the Holy Spirit.

*LUKE 1:56 Mary stayed with Elizabeth for about three months and Then returned home.

*LUKE 1:57 When it was time for Elizabeth to have her baby, she Gave birth to a son.

*LUKE 1:58 On the eighth day they came to circumcise the child, And they were going to name him after his father Zechariah,

LUKE 1:60 But his mother spoke up and said," No! He is to be called John."

LUKE 1:66 Everyone who heard this wondered about it, asking, "What then is this child going to be? "For the Lord's hand was with Him.

*LUKE 1:76 And you, my child, will be called a prophet of the Most High; for you will go on before the Lord to prepare the way for Him,

LUKE 1:77 To give His people the knowledge of salvation through The forgiveness of their sins,

LUKE 1:78 Because of the tender mercy of our God, by which the rising Sun will come to us from heaven.

LUKE 1:79 To shine on those living in darkness and in the shadow Of death, to guide our feet into the path of peace."

LUKE 1:80 And the child grew and became strong in spirit; and he Lived in the desert until he appeared publicly to Israel.

LUKE 2:1 In those days Caesar Augustus issued a decree that a census Should be taken of the entire Roman world.

LUKE 2:4 So Joseph also went up from the town of Nazareth in Galilee To Judea, to Bethlehem the town of David, because he belonged to the House and line of David.

*LUKE 2:5 He went there to register with Mary, who was pledge to be Married to him and was expecting a child.

*LUKE 2:6 While they were there, the time came for the baby to be Born,

*LUKE 2:7 And she gave birth to her firstborn, a son. She wrapped Him in cloth and placed Him in a manger, because there was no room In the inn.

LUKE 2:8 And there were shepherds living out in the fields nearby keeping

Watch over their flocks at night.

LUKE 2:9 An angel of the Lord appeared to them, and the glory of the Lord shone around them, and they were terrified.

LUKE 2:10 But the angel said to them, "Do not be afraid. I bring you good News of great joy that will be for all the people.

LUKE 2:11 Today in the town of David A Savior has been born to you He is Christ the Lord.

LUKE 2:12 "This will be a sign to you: You will find a baby wrapped in Cloths and lying in a manger."

LUKE 2:13 Suddenly a great company of the heavenly host appeared With the angel, praising God saying,

LUKE 2:14 "Glory to God in the highest, and on earth peace to men On whom his favor rests."

LUKE 2:15 When the angels had left them and gone into heaven the Shepherds said to one another, "Let's go to Bethlehem and see this Thing that has happened, which the Lord told us about."

LUKE 2:16 So they hurried off and found Mary and Joseph, and the Baby, who was lying in the manger.

LUKE 2:17 When they had seen him, they spread the word concerning What had been told to them about the child,

LUKE 2:20 The shepherds returned, glorifying and praising God for All the things they had heard and seen, which were just as they had Been told.

*LUKE 2:21 On the eighth day, when it was time to circumcise Him He was named, Yashua/Jesus the name the angel had given Him before He had been conceived.

LUKE 2:22 When the time of their purification according to the Law of Moses had been completed, Joseph and Mary took Him to Jerusalem to present Him to the LORD

LUKE 2:23 As it is written in the Law of the LORD every first born Male is to be consecrated to the LORD"

LUKE 2:24 And offer a sacrifice in keeping with what is said in the Law Of the Lord;" a pair of doves or two young pigeons."

LUKE 2:40 And the child grew and became strong; he was filled with Wisdom, and the grace of God was upon Him.

What I Like About Christmas

To me Christmas is everyday.
When I say everyday.
Christmas is spending time
With the Savior.

Christmas is loving
My brothers and sisters.
Christmas is keeping
The sick in my prayers.

Christmas is blessing
Those who are hungry.
Christmas is visiting
The needy.

Christmas is rejoicing.
Christmas is opening
The gates with Thanksgiving.
Christmas is giving
Yourself to whoever
Needs you.

But the best thing
I like about Christmas
Is the chance to tell
Of His truth.
Not the commercialistic
Ritualistic
Bells and trees.

Truth is June is the month
Not December
That our King was born.
Born to die.
But glorified in resurrection.
The Savior of the world

He's Yashua Jesus
With Him
Everyday is "Christmas."

Beginning, The End
and Everything in Between

My Story
ISAIAH 53:4 Surely He took up our infirmities and carried our sorrows,
Yet considered Him stricken by God, smitten by him, and afflicted.

ISAIAH 53:5 But He was pierced for our transgressions, He was crushed
For our iniquities; the punishment that brought us peace was upon Him,
And by His wounds we are healed.

My Story

If anyone should ever write my life story
Tell them that I have overcome.

Let them know
My life had such meaning.

Let them know
I was true to myself.
I did help others.

Even though they used me
Abuse me, persecuted me
Talk about me, shame me
Talk evil against me, judge me
Hated me without a cause.
Showed their two faced deeds.

Yes! All of this was done to me
But in their wrong doing
I claim the victory.
With all those fiery darts
Thrown at me.
I was able to stay strong
And took everything
That was against me
And build from that.

As the Accuser continue
To use his Disciples.
It's one thing that he
Forgot to tell his own people.
That he's setting them up too.

As he laughed, and say
He to believe in karma.
What goes around

Does come around.

So if anyone should ever
Write my life story.
Tell them this!

She is a woman of God.
She reverence Him.
She feared Him.
She has a relationship with her King.
She loved the Lord with all of her heart.
She was chosen by God.
She's a child of the Most High.
She's adopted into the family ,
Of Isaac, Abraham, and Jacob.
She did overcome.
She did forgive.
She did love.
She took those lashes.
She prayed for her enemies.
She prayed to God for them,
And their ignorance.
She did triumph.

So if anyone should ever
Write my life story.
Know that I did
Heeded to God's call.
For those of you,
Do be careful , who you
Talk against.
Who's name you put in your mouth
For one may never know
Who's anointed by God.

So if anyone should ever
Write my life story
Tell them those things.

Beginning, The End
and Everything in Between

Death To Rebirth
EPHESIANS 6:11 Put on the full armor of God so that you can take your
Stand against the devil schemes.

EPHESIANS 6:12 For our struggle is not against flesh and blood, but
Against the rulers, against the authorities, against the powers of this dark
World and against the spiritual forces of evil in the heavenly realms.

Death To Rebirth

I would never forget that day
The enemy came in an attack my child.
Restless and confuse
Tired and weary unable to fight.

The Accuser knew when to attack
Unable to defend one self.
Yet still she would not give up the fight.
A strong will individual
Was fighting with all her might.

But the Enemy knew
Just how to defeat her.
He enter her mind.
He knew once I get that
Everything else will line up.
So he did just that.

Though confuse she did seem.
The mind is racing.
Taking her in some unfamiliar places.
Seeing unfamiliar things.
Speaking with Babel tongues.
The doctors were confuse too,
Not knowing Why?
They called it this.
They called it that.

But I knew what was happening.
It's Spiritual warfare.
The battle of the mind.
One will never understand,
If you are not walking in the spiritual realm.
Now try to explain that to people ,
Who's thinking carnal minded.
That's a war within it self , and a battle.

So I continue to witness what was going on.
Again , I stated "I knew!"
The battle of the mind.
I fell on my knees.
LORD as I began to pray.
Pleading the blood of Jesus.
Anointing my house , and everything in it.
I called those things out,
And told the Devil to take his hands
Off of my child.

I saw with my spiritual eyes,
And had to take myself in that spiritual place.
Having that talk with my Maker,
As my spirit led me to the book of Job.
I read for I felt like Job.
I knew this is between
God, Me , and the Adversary.
As much as I could've invited others in
I could not , for we had to go through
Those dark moments by ourselves.

As they wanted to keep my child
Longer than she should have stayed.
"I said, No !"
As God was doing his work on her.
He was bringing her through.
The Devil was doing his work too.
"But yes she is a fighter!"

God gave her the spirit of discernment.
He showed her the difference
Between good and evil.
This all took place in the mind.
They were still in unbelief as
The doctors gave this a name
Never willing to give any credit to God

For we know where our deliverance come from

She never claim anything that
They had to say against her.
But she gave Glory to God.
As I continue making intercession
On her behalf.
A mighty work was being done.
As prayer and praise went forth,
And we took one day at a time
Her healing came forth.

For the Devil is a liar.
Touch not God anointed one,
Do his children know harm
We put the Devil under arrest ,
And his unbelievers.

When one is going through.
Know your Creator for yourself.
Have the right people in your corner,
That know how to pray.
Continue praying without ceasing.
Pray until something happens.
Pray with power and authority.
Your healing will come.
Believe and claim your healing,
Though the Anointed One.
Who is Yashua Jesus the Christ
And her rebirth was on 10/25/06

The Beginning , The End And Everything In Between

It Could Be You
1Peter 2:3 When they hurled their insults at him, he did not retaliate; when he suffered , he made no threats. Instead, he entrusted himself to him who judges justly.

It Could Be You

I was out having dinner
With some of my friends.
There were some handsome
Gentlemen having dinner too.
One of the gentlemen and
Myself were seated facing one another.
As I converse with my friends.
I notice him stirring back at me.
I gave him a smile.
He smiled back.
A waiter came over to our table.
"Excuse me, said the waiter!"
The gentlemen at the other table
Want to know, What are you drinking
And eating?
So I told the waiter.
Then the waiter said
Could I take your order?
That gentlemen at the next table
Would like to pay for your meal
And drink.
"So I said wow!"
Tell him thanks.

After dinning out with my friends.
We all were headed to the door.
"Excuse me Ms!"
As the gentlemen introduce himself.
My name is_____
I said please to meet you.
And thank you sir again
For the meal and drink.
Sure he said, that's not a problem.
Is it alright , if I give you my phone number
He asked?.
I said sure sir!
We talked to each other on the

Telephone just about everyday.
We went on dates with our friends.
He introduce me to his family.
I introduce him to mine.
We couldn't get enough of each other.
He showered me with so many gifts.
We were beginning to fall in love.
He called me everyday.
He picked me up from work everyday.
So, we've been together for five years now.
Then we decided to get engage.
We were engage for one year.
My gentlemen said that he was ready now.
Then we planned the day
That we were going to get married.

Well a year later.
We did just that.
Talking about adoring one another.
He is the love of my life.
One day I went to work.
My boss called me into his office.
He offered me another job position.
This job paid more money than I
Am making right now.
"Excite!" I said yes.
I will take the job.
This made me happy.
I couldn't wait to go home
To share the good news with my husband.

It was time to leave my job for today.
Now it's time for me to go home .
I can't wait to share the good news!"
Pulling up to my driveway.
I opened the door.
As I called him.
"Honey, I'm home!"
I have some good news to share

With you.
As my husband walked from the kitchen.
He asked, What is it?
"I said honey, my boss offered me a
New job position!"
It pays more money, than the job
I had before.
All of a sudden.
His hand went up.
"Slap, as his hand went across my lips."
The blood came screaming down my mouth.
I asked, Why did you do that?
Again his hand went up.
"Smack across my face."
He yelled shut up!
Don't say anything else.
So I didn't say a word.
"He yelled, Women
Now you listen to me."
If any man offer you anything
You check with me first.
You let me decide to tell you what to do.
You are my women.
You belong to me.
You go back and tell your boss
That you won't be taking that job.
I said but honey.
This will help us to catch up
On some bills.
Again his hand went up.
Did I tell you to talk?
He hit me in the face.
This time with a closed fist.
I ran.
He caught me.
"Oh women you done mess up now."
Don't you ever run away from me.
Again he punch and hit me.

He was beating me down.
As if he was fighting a man.
My beating was almost everyday.
"Where will he hit me today?"
If it's not my face.
I'm getting head shoots.
If it's not the head shoots.
I'm getting blows to my body.
If it's not the blows to my body.
I'm getting push down the stairs.
If I'm not getting push down the stairs.
I'm getting whipped with a belt.
If I'm not getting whipped with a belt.
I'm getting slammed down to the floor.
If I'm not getting slammed down to the floor.
I'm getting kick in my kidney.
If I'm not getting kick in my kidney.
I'm getting called everything , but a child of God.
If I'm not getting called everything , but a child of God.
I'm getting locked in my room.
If I'm not getting locked in my room.

I'm getting violated repeatedly.
If I'm not getting violated repeatedly.
I'm getting drag across the floor.
If I'm not getting drag across the floor.
I'm getting dishes thrown at me.
If I'm not getting dishes thrown at me.
I'm getting choke.
If I'm not getting choke.
I'm getting spit in my face.
If I'm not getting spit in my face.
I'm getting insulted by his friends.
If I'm not getting insulted by his friends.
I'm getting my hair pulled.
If I'm not getting my hair pulled.
I'm getting a busted nose.
If I'm not getting a busted nose.

I'm getting squeeze almost to death.
"Oh my God!
What will it be today?
My body has been subjected
To all this abuse.
He has done everything to me.
"Oh yes", I forgot.
He Hasn't Killed Me Yet!

The Beginning, The End and Everything in Between

Patience
Psalm104:4 Look to the Lord and his strength; seek His face always.

Patience

We are a family of nine,
And we love each other.
My husband has to be
At work four a.m. in the morning.

I am up at six a.m.;
Preparing breakfast for my family.
The oldest child is twenty-two
The youngest is eight.
Two of my oldest children,
Were bless to go off to college.
Only by God's grace.
While five of our children are at home.
My husband is a hard working man.
He's doing the best that he can.

I work for this big Corporation.
I started from the bottom,
And worked my way to a supervisor position.
At least I thought , it was a supervisor position.
My boss promise me a pay raise that came
Along with that position.
At my job, I have trained more and more
Temps that came from different agencies.
I had to be at work at eighty-thirty in the morning.
I was suppose to get off at five-thirty.
Of course that never happened.
Because my boss asked for more and more of me.
After training other people
My work get neglected,
Causing me to work overtime.
It is now eight thirty at night.
My children are home alone.
Because my husband worked from four a.m.
Until his job is through with him.

As I shut off my computer

And walked to my car.
I called my children from my cell phone.
My seventeen year old said to me.
"Well Mama the cable is turned off."
And the house is cold again.
I think that we are out of oil.
There is nothing in the house to eat.
Your eight year old is catching a cold.
Your fourteen year old is acting up in school.
Your sixteen year was brought home by the police.
And your twelve year old has a boyfriend.
"Oh ", the gas and electric man came to
Turn off your lights.
But I pleaded with him, and told him that we
Have a sick grandmother in the house ,who
Needed our undivided attention.
"Hello!, Hello!, Hello!" , Mama are you still there?
Yes baby I am here.
I'm on my way home.
I'll talk to you more, when I get there.
"Lord help!"
What am I to do?
As I arrived home.
Put the key in the door.
The house was cold.
The cable was off.
There was no food on the stove.
My eight year old had a runny nose.
My twelve year old was on the telephone
Talking to her boyfriend.
My fourteen year old handed me a letter
For dentition.
My sixteen year old was brought home by
The police for vandalizing someone property.
My seventeen year old is doing the best that
She can.
I talked to myself as I prayed from within.
"Lord I need your help"!

I looked inside the cabinets.
I found two potatoes , box of rice, can of tomato
And a box of cornbread.
"I told my children , this is tonight dinner."
My fourteen year old yelled out!
But Mama what about tomorrow?
I said to him.
My son tomorrow has it's own set of problems.
Let me worry about today.
After dinner was cooked and served.
I knew that I had to do something.
I told my children that I would be right back.

I walked down to my aunt house.
Who lived one block from me.
I knock on her door.
She was happy to see me.
We talked for awhile.
I asked to borrow some money
From her, until I get paid.
I told her that we have no food.
The lights will be turned off soon.
The house has no heat.
My aunt said to me,
"Oh ", I am so sorry baby.
But I have nothing to give you.
What I would do is keep you in my prayer.
I said thanks to my aunt and walked out
The door.
As I walked down the street
With tears in my eyes , with a heavy heart.
I opened my mouth again.
"Lord help me!"
As I was getting closer to my house.
I dried my eyes.
And opened the door.
My children asked.
"Mama where did you go?"
I went for a walk, that's what I told them.

"Then I said children get ready for bed!"
There was a knock at the door.
It was a friend of my husband.
He asked, was my husband at home.
I said no.
Then he spoke.
Give this hundred dollars
To your husband.
He loaned fifty dollars to me
Two months ago.
Sorry that it took me so long to
Pay him back.
But I added an extra fifty dollars in.
Tell your husband thanks my sister,
And for being a good friend.
I said you are welcome.
Then I closed the door.
"I yelled, thank you Jesus!"
I ran to the telephone to call
My husband.
I told him about my day.
And all of what was going on.
My husband gave me some
Encouraging words.
Baby trust in the Lord,
And lean not on your own understanding.
You take that hundred dollar,
And buy some groceries.
Don't worry about the heat,
The children, leave that to me.
I'm on my way home.
Go pray and rest.

The next day. I was at work.
It was a job position that I
Applied for six months ago.
After training all the temps
That came from agencies.
They learned their jobs.

It was this particular young girl
That I trained.
Mind you , she is the new kid on the block.
So she went up for the same position.
I am more experience for this position
Than she.
And I put in the years.
My boss did interview both of us for the position.
I was walking to the water fountain.
I over heard the temp that I trained,
Telling her friend that she has the position.
I stormed to my boss office.
How could this be?
I am more qualified for that position than she!
That girl has only been on this job for six months.
What's up with that?
Was it her big breast, small waist
That hour glass figure.
Those long fake eyelashes that she batted at you.
Or was it her long flowing hair.
You tell me!
She still need more training with the position
That she is already in.
Again I asked, What's up with that?
My boss said back to me calmly.
You do a good job in training
The temps that come in.
"I yelled again!"
And where is the pay that came with
That supervisor position?
While I was on a roll.
I yelled again!
Where is my raise?
My boss look at me, and spoke again.
You are good at training
The temps that come in.
I stormed out of his office.
I finish doing my work

Until it was time to go home.
"Finally this day is over!"

I ran to my car .
I cried out to the Lord.
"I don't understand!"
From my spirit , I heard
Those who are last,
Will be first.
I answered , but Lord I am
The only one who is left at
That work place.
Everyone else quit.
The Spirit of the Lord spoke again.
You are the last and only one
Who remained at that Corporation.
My child do not fret.
When I was hungry.
They didn't feed Me.
When I was thirsty
No one gave Me nothing to drink.
When I was in the hospital
No one came to see Me.
When I was in prison
No one came to visit Me.
The least they did unto you.
The did unto Me.
Finally I understood.
I dried my eyes.
I praise the Lord all the more.
And I thanked Him.

I went to the grocery store.
Then I went home.
I greeted my family,
My husband took care of
The gas and electric bill.
There was oil in the tank,

And my husband had a talk
With the children.

The next day I went back to work.
I had a smile on my face.
I congratulate the temp on
Her new position.
My boss walked by me,
And said good morning.
"I said praise the Lord!"
He turned back and looked at me.
He stood still.
He didn't move for about ten minutes.
I kept on smiling.
And did what I do best.
Training the temps as they came in.
My boss called me in his office.
He said that, he created
A new position for me.
It pays twice as much as
The job that I have.
And the one that I applied for.
He wanted me to be the spokes person
For his Corporation , to show other
Workers and Supervisors;
How you suppose to train workers.
When they come to work for big Corporation.
How to stay with the Corporation.
My boss thank me for turning
His Corporation around.
"Excite! I excepted the new position.
Glory Hallelujah ,
And To
God Be the Glory!

The Beginning , The End and Everything In Between

Breaking Bread

Psalm 64:5 They encourage each other in evil
Plans , they talk about hiding their snares ;
They say , "Who will see them ?

Psalm 64:6 They plot injustice and say ,
"We have devised a perfect plan !"
Surely the mind and heart of man are
Cunning.

Proverbs 4:14 Do not set foot on the path
Of the wicked or walk in the way of evil
Men.

Proverbs 4:15 Avoid it , do not travel on
It; turn from it and go on your way .

Proverbs 4;16 For they cannot sleep till
They do evil ; they are robbed of slumber
Till they make someone fall .

Proverbs 4:17 They eat the bread of wickedness
And drink the wine of violence .

Proverbs 4:18 The path of the righteous is like
The first gleam of dawn , shining ever brighter
Till the full light of day .

Proverbs 4:19 But the way of the wicked is
Like deep darkness ; they do not know what
Makes them stumble .

Proverbs 4:20 My son pay attention to what
I say ; listen closely to my words .

Proverbs 4:21 Do not let them out of your
Sight ; keep them within your heart;

Proverbs 4:22 For they are life to those who
Find them and health to a man's whole body .

Proverbs 4:23 Above all else , guard your heart,
For it is the wellspring of life .

Proverbs 4:24 Put away perversity from your
Mouth ; keep corrupt talk far from your lips.

Proverbs 4:25 Let your eyes look straight ahead,
Fix your gaze directly before you .

Proverbs 4:26 Make level paths for your feet
And take only ways that are firm.

Proverbs 4:27 Do not swerve to the right or the
Left ; keep your foot from evil .

Proverbs 6:12 A scoundrel and villain , who
Goes about with a corrupt mouth ,

Proverbs 6:13 Who winks his eyes , signals
With his feet and motions with his fingers,

Proverbs 6:14 Who plots evil with deceit in
His heart – he always stirs up dissension .

Proverbs 6:15 Therefore disaster will overtake
Him in an instant; he will suddenly be destroyed
Without remedy .

Proverbs 6:16 There are six things the LORD
Hates, seven that are detestable to Him;

Proverbs 6:17 Haughty eyes, a lying tongue,
Hands that shed innocent blood,

Proverbs 6:18 A heart that devises wicked schemes,
Feet that are quick to rush into evil ,

Proverbs 6:19 A false witness who pours out lies
And a man who stirs up dissension among brothers .

Breaking Bread

It was close to the holiday .
So my department decided to have
A celebration .
Ms Judas who happened to be one
Of my co-workers.
She agreed to bring in several dishes.
"So we said okay Ms Judas!"
And left it as that .

Ms Judas went to another department
Located on the second floor.
She discuss what we were going to do .
Ms Judas suggested that they do the
Same thing too.
She offered to bring several dishes.
"So we said okay Ms Judas!"
And left it as that.

Ms Judas went to the Human Resource
Department.
To discuss what the second floor was
Going to do .
She suggested that they do the same thing
Too .
She offered to bring several dishes .
"So we said okay Ms Judas!"
And left it as that.

Ms Judas went to the last department
That happen to be on the bottom floor.
She discuss what the Human Resource
Department was going to do .
She offered to bring several dishes.
"So we said okay Ms Judas !"
And left it as that.

So at the end of the day .
Ms Judas spoke to one of her coworker from
The first floor.
Ms Judas said "Don't you know that you know
Who from the bottom floor was talking about all
Of your coworker on your floor."
She said that it was their idea of having the
Holiday celebration, and why are they trying
To turn it around like it was their idea?
And another thing, you know "she said."
Why am I allowing you all to use me ?

Then Ms Judas caught up with another coworker
On the second floor .
Ms Judas said, "Don't you know that you know
Who is mad at you from the first floor.
"She said, how could you all steal their idea
About the holiday celebration, and why are
All the coworkers were having it on the same
Day as theirs?

Next, Ms Judas saw another coworker from
The third floor .
Ms Judas said, " Don't you know that you
Know who from the second floor was talking
About you all .
She said that you all think your floor is better
Then theirs.

Finally, Ms Judas saw another coworker from
The bottom floor.
Ms Judas said " Don't you know you know
Who on the third floor is jealous of all of you."

Ms Judas is finish with all of her rounds.
She talked with her coworkers from each floor.
She talked about one to another .
Ms Judas make herself look good so it seem.

After her day had ended.
Ms Judas stopped to visit some friends.
It was supper time .
They insisted that Ms Judas stay and
Break bread with them.
So Ms Judas did just that .

They had some deep conversation .
Ms Judas was part of that conversation.
One of the coworker at Ms Judas place
Of employment was breaking bread too.

They laughed, they talk, and had a nice
Time breaking bread one to another.
It was time to leave .

Ms Judas called another coworker
From her cell phone .
Ms Judas told one coworker about another
Coworker .
Girl, watch what you say around her .
"She is no one friend, all that time,
I thought she like you ."
With friends like that, who need enemies.
I have to go now.
I will talk to you later.

Ms Judas went home to prepare all of
Her dishes, that she promise to bring
To the holiday celebration .

The next day come .
The coworker were all
 Mad at each other.
The first floor was
Mad at the second floor.

The second floor was
Mad at the third floor.
And the third floor
was mad at the bottom floor.
It was a mess, chaos was all around.

Finally, someone with some
Wisdom spoke out.
"Where did all this backbiting and bickering
Come from?
They said from Ms Judas!
Wisdom spoke, "Now there you have it .
Let us wait for Ms Judas.

Ms Judas loaded up her car.
With all the dishes
That she promise to bring.
Tragedy, Ms Judas was no more.
Her life came to an end .

**The Beginning The End
and Everything In Between**

The King Of Glory
PSALMS 24:10 Who is He , this King Of Glory ?
The LORD Almighty – He is The King Of Glory .

The King Of Glory

Tired and sick and tired
Of being sick and tired .
With so much trivial non sense .
Non sense that made
No sense .
All it was , is a bunch of nuisance.

It was so much negative energy.
Sucking you up like a vapor .
Trying to take you back to some
Unfamiliar places.

The Enemy whisper in your ear.
You're not worthy!
You're not worthy!
You're not worthy!

After hearing this from the enemy
So many times.
You would think that you aren't worthy .
As you allow that deadly tune to
Play in your head .
It had you believing that, you're not worthy.
You may have felt that you weren't
Worthy to call on His name .
But cheer up!
For your are worthy.
I say this to you .
Cry Out!
Then this is what you will hear .
Who is He ? This King Of Glory .
The LORD Almighty , He is the King Of Glory .

Your heart may seem heavy at time.
You may feel like giving up .

Trouble may come
When you least
Expect it .
Your friends may betray you .
You may be facing a divorce .
The enemy is trying to take your seed .
Your children may have disappointed you .
You may had a hard time keeping a job .
Whatever your plot may be .
Just remember He .

Who is He ? This King Of Glory.
The LORD Almighty , He is The King Of Glory .
This will make you feel so much better .
I am a testimony .
With all those plots that came into my
Life .
He didn't leave me there .
As I surrender all unto Him .
He showed me that I still had
A chance to the Tree Of Life .

So if the Enemy come and whisper
In your ear again, say this to him .
The LORD , The LORD .
He is The King Of Glory .
He is and will always be .
So Devil just leave .
For He has come and set
The captives free.

The Beginning The End
and Everything in Between

The Man
ISAIAH 48:12 "Listen to me, O Jacob, Israel, whom I have called:
I Am the First and I Am the Last.

ISAIAH 48:13 My own hand laid the foundation of the earth, and my
Right hand spread out the heavens; when I summon them, they all stand
Up together.

The Man

He is The Man
The Man in my life.
I put Him first before anyone.
This Man has brought great joy
Into my life.

He is my Shield and Protection.
He is with me everyday.
I can't get enough of Him.

He woke me up in this morning.
As the Sun is all ready shining.
He is the One behind that.
When the garden needed to be
Attended too.
He is behind that.
After the hot scorching weather
With the temperature around
One hundred degrees.
He sent down His rain.

This Man know what I need
At the right time when I need it.

The Man in my life.
Talk with me about
Everyday life.

My Man should me how to
Pick and chose my battle.
And when I do chose my battle.
My Man would be the One
Who's directing me.

My Man is the head and Center
Of my life.

I have eyes for Him only.
We have been together for so long.
My Man shape me into His image.
We look so much alike.
I call Him my twin.
Whatever He do.
I find myself doing the same thing too.
When He walk.
I walk.
When He talk.
I talk.
When He corrects.
I find myself doing the same thing too.

My Man had to separate Himself from
Others who want nothing to do with Him.
I find myself doing that too.
My Man should me how to pray
For those who talk evil against you.
Now I am doing that too.
My Man is always encouraging me.
So now I am doing that too.
My Man is so contagious.
That I caught that too.
My Man said to me.
Whatever you see Me do.
You will do it too.

My man followed His Father.
For he is His Father's Son.
I am His daughter.
Now the three of us are one.
My man left this with me.
I am in my Father.
And my Father is in me.
You are my Father's daughter.
So we are three.
This union that we have together.

Never let it be broken.

I am the man.
But my Father is The Man.
We left you the spirit.
So do as we do.
He's Spirit.
I'm Spirit.
You're spirit.
We're spirit.

So my Father left
You the Holy Spirit.
He is your teacher.
My love your man
Who you call the man.
Will still be the only man
In your life.

So continue to praise your man.
So others would look up to
This man.
Who is The Man.
The Center of your life.

The Beginning The End
and Everything In Between

Dreams
HABAKUK 2:2-3 "Write down the revelation and make it
Plan on tablets so that a herald may run with it .

For the revelation awaits an appointed time ; It speaks of
The end and will not prove false .
Through it linger , wait for it , It will certainly come and
Will not delay .

Dreams

They said you are a dreamer .
Who in the hell will listen to you.
No one believe in you .
The only dream I see you having .
Is in a fairy tale book .

Never listen to them .
For dream do come true .
I have a dream .
And so do you .
Keep on believing
For your dreams will
Come true.
Keep on preserving
For that dream do
Live inside of you .

Never give up !
What God has deposit
Inside of you .
Reach for your tomorrow .
Plan carefully , write it down .
And make it plain and simple .
Don't listen to the Nay Sayers.

Continue to go to God
With your prayers.
Make your request
Known to Him .
He know you from the beginning .
Your life has been predestine by Him.
So dreamer , dream big .
Bigger than you can ever imagine .
May your dreams become an reality .
God know something , what the Nay

People, "Said that could never
happened."
Yahweh know more than they do .
For your life is predestine
Continue to dream .
While God will be the One
Who will bless you
And your dreams.
So dream
Dream big
Bigger than
You could ever imagine.

The Beginning , The End
And Everything In Between

Therapy
1JOHN 3:9-10 No one who is born of God will continue to
Sin because God's seed remains in him ; he cannot go on
Sinning , because he has been born of God .

This is how we know who the children of God are and the
Children of the devil are : Anyone who does not do what is
Right is not a child of God; nor is anyone who does not love
His brother .

Therapy

What do you call therapy ?
How will you view therapy ?
Are you in therapy
Because of you ?
Or is it because of someone else ?
With all those trivial nonsense
Going on in today's world .
It's a wonder that we all
Aren't in therapy .
But how could we turn our
Heads and walk away .
We see crazy- ness on the news all day .
We have confusion right in our own home .
Hate in our heart from generation curses .
Teaching it to our seed .
Don't hang around him or her!
Because they think their better than me .
Or maybe it's never about you !
It's all about them .
Hoping that they will never be called out .
So they take all the focus away from self.
But Oh !!!!
"Do be careful."
Please put on your spiritual beamer .
If the gossiper is telling you about them .
What are they saying about you ?
Are you in therapy, because of you?
Or is it because of someone else.

So much trivial nonsense
In today's world .
But there is hope .
When the Accuser come to you about
Someone else .

"Excuse yourself .

"Protect your ears .
"Guard your heart .
"Separate yourself .
When the Accuser come at you in
Another way .
"Oh yes, he will come back!"
If he continue where he left off .
Invite him in .
Be polite to him .
Then you excuse yourself.
Tell him that you will be right back .
You heard a knock at the door .
Introduce your invited company .
That the Accuser brought accusation against .
Say to him/she.
Now Mr./Ms finish telling me what you
Have to say about them .
While your invited company
Is standing there.

"So, all the therapy you need
Is all inside of you .
You are more intelligent than that.
Watch what you say .
And know who you are talking too .
Choose the company you keep
Very wisely .
You see the Accuser come in many disguises.

He pretends to be a friend .
He will use you, until he gets what he want .
Yes he even praises the Lord too .
He's been to church too .
He even goes on Sunday .
He sings on church choirs .
He even has his own followers .
He preach in the Pull Pit from time to time .
He even goes to family functions .

He loves to gossip on the telephone .
He may even start back associating with
Some long lost relatives .
He has many disciples .
He taught them how to run to and fro .
Once his game has come to an end .
You will find out that
The Accuser just use you .
He will have you in therapy .
And in a web of mess .
Not because of something you did .
But for what he did to you .
All I am saying is
"Brethren"!!!
You have to watch
Who 's entertaining who.
Put on your spiritual beamers .
Do what I'm telling you !
If you don't feel right .
Then it's not right .

Stop allowing the Accuser to come in .
Resist him, he will flee .
Then dropped on your knees .
Pray and asked God for forgiveness .
Because you partake with the
Accuser foolishness .
You are more guilty than he .
Because you paid so much attention to him.
He's pointing a finger at you too .
Now you see how easy he suckered you.
You entertain him .
You gave him a stage .
Now he's bad mouthing you .
The two of you, broke bread together .
Now who's doing what to who ?

My Brethren !!!!!!

You see
We all are in this plot .
But we don't have to be .
Think with wisdom .
Stop being so noisy .
Think with wisdom .
What does light have to do with dark ?
What does good have to do with evil ?
Do oil and water go together ?
What does positive have to do with negative ?
What does faith have to do with doubt ?
"Brethren "
Do you hear me ?
Let me put it to your this way .
Don't hear me .
Hear Him !
"Our Creator .
Let the wise listen and add to their learning
And let the discerning get guidance .
The fear of the LORD is the beginning of
Knowledge, but fools despise wisdom and
Discipline .
So come out from them !
Before you find yourself needing much therapy .
Not from what you did,
Maybe because of someone else .

My Brethren!
Yashua Jesus is all the therapy you need .
If you will yourself to Him .
He will make you free .
He and God knows what's in a man's heart .
Give it to them .
You gave it to the Accuser .
How easy was that .

My Brethren !
Keep your spiritual snuffer on .

When the Accuser show up again .
"Stop him /her/ them .
And turn away .

Give praises to the Lord .
Give Him your attention .
Tell Him all about it .
Then you will see .
His therapy is free .
It cost you nothing .
But it cost Him his life .
He is the Therapy .
That we all need .

The Beginning The End
and Everything in Between

Position
PSALM 82:2 How long will Ye judge unjustly, and accept the person
Of the wicked? Selah

PSALM 82:3 Defend the poor and fatherless do justice to the afflicted
And needy.

PSALM 82:4 Deliver the poor and needy rid them out of the hand of
The wicked.

Position

The battle of Armageddon
Is getting ready for preparation
Do you watch television?
Wars and rumors of wars.
Did you look outside of your windows?
Gangs against gangs.
Look in your communities
They are coming soon
Don't turn away
They are on the prey
The evil spirit is looking
He's searching
Please don't become his prey.
Don't do it!
Prison are overcrowded
Don't get caught in the mix
Stop! Think, don't trip
Don't do what that person did to you
Stop, think, walk away!
Don't let a Judge and jury trialed you
Think about the situation
Before they have to do, what they do.
Woe! But you didn't.
You just would not listen.
Now shackles are on your hands and feet.
Repeating history past
Shame on you!
Did you stop to think about your
Forefathers and mothers?
Who was force to have shackles.
From past history
This should not be
Brethren please stop repeating history.
Don't shame yourself
Your life is so much precious than that.
No one may never told you

That you are Kings and Queens.
You are Royalty
You are Ambassadors
You are made in His image

Don't take on the Accuser identity
He created identity theft
He hates his self
He is so insecure
He hides behind others
So they could do his dirty work
He regroups
He calls his troops
He's a coward
"There he goes again, calling
On others to do his dirty work!
He has set the mark

STOP!
"Wait one minute!"
Do this seem familiar?
We see it in on our streets
Gangs against gangs
Making themselves seem bigger it seems.
Grabbing our babies at such a tender age.
This should not be!
Did you stop to asked.
Where did it all started from?

Newsflash:
Spy through the book of
Genesis 3:1-4
Isaiah 14:12 Say:
How you have fallen from heaven,
O morning star, son of dawn!
You have been cast down to the earth,
You who once laid low the nations!
Then old Lucifer tongue became so boastful

With the I will.

Isaiah 14:13 and 14:14 Says:
I will ascend to heaven;
I will raise my throne
Above the stars of God;
I will sit enthroned on the
Mount of assembly, on the
Utmost heights of the sacred mountain.
I will ascend above the tops of the clouds
I will make myself like the Most High

But the Most High kick him out of heaven
Him and a third of the angels
Woe! He is on his prey
He runs to and fro
Looking for souls so he could deposit
His spirit inside of them
You see he's a liar
He's a trickster
He knows what he like
Yes! He likes bling
The material things
The platinum
The sliver
The gold
The diamonds
The furs
The cars
The mansion
The money
The titles
The contracts
The credit cards
The latest cell phone
With the ring –a- tone.
You know all the latest stuff
Yes! He knows what you like

He likes it too
But if you cross him
He will send his entourage after you
See in his world
He look at it this way
You both have so much in common
What a comparison!
His disciples
Your dawgs
His accusers
Your peeps
His adversary
Your boys
Some call him Lucifer
Some call you Big Lucky
Some call him Satan
Some call you Judas
Some call him Devil
Some call you Clever
Some call him Serpent
Some call you Boss Man

Get the picture!
He chose you
He make it look so good

But Wait!
You can out smart him
Just say **No**
Jesus did
When He was tempted
By the Devil
You can learn to say that
Beautiful word **No**
Go ahead it's easy
"Say it."
No! No! No! No! No! No! No!
Mean what you say

Think about what you do!

When the Devil or Mr. Clever
Come and force themselves on you
Don't give them a stage
Walk away, walk away, walk away!

Replace your negative energy
With positive thoughts, things, and friends.

Satan don't like you
So you shouldn't like him
Have love for the **One**
Who created you
If you don't know about Him
Start with Genesis 1:26 to 1:27
Then read the gospels of
Mathew
Mark
Luke
John
They were Yashua Jesus disciples
They talk all about the Messiah
The **One** who laid down His life
For you and me
Brethren choose life
Don't die for your hommies
You and the adversary
Already know what those
Streets look like
Do something a little different
"Fit to get out, Not In
You can turn it around
Be a leader
Become like Jesus
He led by example
Now people are worshipping
And praising Him

Put Him first and watch Him
Make things happen
He won't disappoint you
Not like the enemy will
He came to kill, steal, and destroy
Then leave you in a world of confusion
But it don't have to be
Keep saying and practicing
The word **No!**

It's a positive word
A respectful word
A leadership word
A beautiful word

So the next time you
Have to choose
Stop! Think about it,
And learn this beautiful
Powerful word **No!**
Then you could feel,
You can see,
Those chains being
Release and fallen
To the floor.
You should be proud
And happy.
Because you are your
Own leader which
You were called to be
That King
That Queen
That Ambassador
That Joint Heir
That God made you to be
He put Jesus in Position
To set the captive free.

The Beginning, The End
And Everything In Between

He Will Humble

DEUTERONOMY 8:3 And He humbled you and let you hunger and fed you With manna, which you did not know, nor did your father know; that He Might make you know that man does not live by bread alone, but that man Lives by everything that proceeds out of the mouth of the LORD .

DERTERONOMY 8:5 Know then in your heart that, as a man disciplines his son, the LORD your God disciplines you.

He Will Humble

He will humble ,when He's done you will
    Praise Him
    Exalt Him
    Glorify Him
Because everything He does is right.
All His ways are just
Those who walk in pride
He is able to humble.
When He is done you will
    Praise Him
    Exalt Him
    Glorify Him
Like Nebuchadnezzar
He had to lift up his eyes toward heaven
And realize who gets the glory.

He changed his I
To Your will LORD
Yes heaven rules
It is You who should be
    Praise
    Exalted,
    And Glorify

You are the Most High
I honored and glorified You forever and ever
    I Praise You
    I Exalt You
    I Glorify You
His dominion is an eternal dominion
Nebuchadnezzar said! His Kingdom endures from
Generation to generation
All the people of the earth are regardless as nothing
He does what He pleases, with the powers of heaven
And the people of the earth
No one can hold back His hand or say to Him

What have You done?
He will humble you, when He is done you will
     Praise Him
     Exalt Him
     Glorify Him

He will humble the pride
Those who walk in pride
He is able to humble
When God blesses you
Do recognize who put you there
It's not I, Me, nor Mine, but it is He.

The Beginning, The End
and Everything in Between

Secrets

Ecclesiastes 3:7 A time to tear and a time to mend, a time to be silent and a time to speak

Secrets

You have a secret .
I have a secret .
We all have a secret .
Tell me!
What's your secret?
For Instance :
Can you go back and
Think of the time of
Your innocence.
Do you remember what was
Going on in your family.
When your father slap
Your mother across the face.
Whipped you, your brother
And sister for no reason.
"Then said I dare you to tell."
What goes on in this house
Stay in this house.
If I hear anything about this.
Ya'll better watch out!

You have a secret.
I have a secret.
We all have a secret.
"Tell me!"
What's your secret?
Here's Another
Remember the time
When it was just you and your mother.
Then your mother meet a new friend.
She paid you less attention
And gave all of her undivided
Attention to her new friend.
"Well mother new friend just wanted
It to be only him and her.
So he started bringing up all kind
Of accusation against you.

Mother believe every word that
He said.
Her new friend started putting
His hands on you and encourage
Your mother to participate.
Daily they did this to you.
Then had the nerve to say
What goes on in this house
Stay in this house.
I dare you to say anything.
And if we hear a word of this
You better watch out!

You have a secret.
I have a secret.
We all have a secret.
Tell me!
What's your secret?
Oh , here's another : .
You were at school
And needed some assistance
From a teacher.
"You ask a question?"
About an assignment
Then the teacher reach out
And groped you.
"SHHHHH!" ,don't tell nobody.
What would you do?

You have a secret.
I have a secret.
We all have a secret.
Tell me!
What's your secret?
Oh yes there is more.
Uncle you know
Come over to the house
Just about everyday.
Sat at your table breaking

Bread with your family.
Having drinks with your father.
Not one, two , maybe three or four.
They both were intoxicated.
Your father said , that he had to
Lay down .
Uncle you know who.
Started following you around.
Then he had you pinned in a corner.
Yes he did an awful thing.
You screamed as loudly as you could.
Your father was so drunk .
He couldn't hear a thing.
"Yeah", uncle you know who said
I dare you to tell.
If I hear a word of this
You better watch out!

You have a secret.
I have a secret.
We all have a secret.
Tell me!
What's your secret?
Did you thought that I was done?
Oh here another one.
My credit cards are all max out.
But I do look cute though.
Everybody complemented me on
How good I look.
I wear nothing but designer clothes.
I drive the name brand car.
My house is so big, with the three
Door car garage.
I entertain every weekend.
I like to be the center of attention.
I give just to be giving.
Yes everyone loves me.
"Yet " , I ask me , Do I love myself?
I worried about what other thought of me.

Hum , I wonder if I tell them
My secret.
I have no money.
My car is on the repo list.
I go to bed hungry at night.
I'm about to loose my house.
My designer clothes are all stolen
Because my credit cards are all max out.
I can't afford to pay them.
I' m living pay check to pay check.
Yes I could go on.
So tell me!
What's your secret?
I left the next page blank for you.
I know you could think of one.
Or , if not one
Maybe two or three.
You know
You don't have to tell me.
But do tell yourself.
You have a secret.
I have a secret.
We all have a secret.

Secrets

The names of God

In mainstream Christian usage , "God (capital G) functions as proper noun ; that is , it is a personal name , belonging to one being only , which draws into itself all the thoughts that the biblical names and descriptions of God express .

The main names of God in the OT , all proclaiming aspects of his nature and His link with mankind , are these:

i.   El , Eloah , Elohim , and El Elyon .

ii.   El Elyon (God most high'). These names convey The thought of a transcendent being , superhumanly strong And with inexhaustible life in himself depends .

iii.   Adonay ('Lord; kyrois in LXX) . This means one who Rules over everything external to Him .

iv.   Yahweh ('the LORD ' in AV (KJV) , RV, RSV , NIV, Following kyrios in LXX , Yahweh Sebaoth ('Lord of (heavenly , angelic) hosts).'Yahweh is God's Personal name for Himself , by which His people were to Invoke Him as the Lord who had taken them into covenant With Himself in order to do them good . When God first Stated this name to Moses at the burning bush , He Explained it as meaning 'I Am what I Am , or perhaps most accurately 'I will be what I will be .

v.   More names of God

1. The LORD The God
2. God of Abraham
3. God of Isaac
4. God of Jacob
5. The LORD The God of The Hebrews
6. The LORD The God of Israel
7. LORD is God
8. The LORD
9. God and Father
10. Abba (Father)
11. LORD Almighty

12. Jehovah
13. Jehovah Jireh
14. LORD
Exodus 3:14-18 , 1Chronicles 15:14 , Joshua 22:34,
Joshua 24:14-15 , Isaiah 9:6 Galatians 1:4 , Galatians 4:6

God Just Is:

God is everything . In the beginning God created the heavens and earth . God created living creatures according to their kind . God created man in His own image . In the image of God He created male and female He created them. (Genesis 1:1 , Genesis 1:24 , Genesis 1:27) .

God is self-existent, self-sufficient and self-sustaining

God does not have it in Him , either in purpose or in Power , to stop existing; He exists necessarily with no need of help and support from us (Acts 17:23-25). This is the quality of having life in and from Himself . God is simple , perfect and immutable . These words affirm that He is wholly and entirely involved in everything that He is and does . His nature , goals , plans and ways of acting do not change . God cannot become better of for the worse .

God is infinite , bodiless a Spirit , omnipresent , omniscient , and eternal . These words affirm that God is not bound by any of the limitations of space or time that apply to us. God is always present everywhere , though invisibly and imperceptibly , and is at every moment cognizant of all that ever was , is ,or shall be . He is all of that.

God is purposeful , all powerful , and sovereign in relation to His world . God has a plan for the history of the Universe , and in executing it . He governs and controls all created realities . God acts in , with and through His creatures so as to do everything that He wishes to do exactly as He wishes to do it . By this overruling action .

God achieves His pre-set goals . God had foreordained everything that comes to pass . For the LORD Almighty Is the One you are to regard as Holy.

The next day I felt a little better. My fever was gone. It was time for the doctors to make their rounds. When they came to my room. They said that I was a sick young lady, that I made it just in time. "Again to GOD be the Glory! It was time to eat, but I had no appetite. The visiting hours came, and my family are here to see me. I had no color, still weak, not looking my best. It felt like I was having a heart attack. My family was very concern. They spoke to the doctors. The doctors said that they were doing all they could. The visiting hours were over. My family went home. The nurse came in my room, and took all the I.V. off of me. I was able to get out of the bed , so I sat at the bottom of my bed. I prayed to GOD so hard. I prayed to GOD to heal my body. As the nurse enter back into the room. She dared not to disturb me. I was praying without ceasing. When I was through . I get up, went to bed and retired for that night.

It's Sunday morning . I turned the television on TBN Station. Their was a Pastor by the name of Pastor Brown. He said that their is a lady right now in the hospital who has pneumonia. He said that I know you are watching. Place your hands on the television, while I pray for you. I did just that. Believing and stepping out on faith .I felt better. I ate breakfast, shower while my linen was being changed. Later the nurse walked in the room , and said that I could go home on tomorrow. "I said alright!" I called my family to tell them the news. It was getting late and time for me to go to bed.

Morning came and it was time for me to go home. I was given a tube to blow through. An albuterol inhaler to use as needed. Instruction not to lay down flat in the bed, to sit in an upward position to protect my lungs. This would help me to breath better. I was picked up from the hospital by family members. While at home. My breathing was very difficult. I was having attacks. I could only walk but a short distance. I was tired. My breathing was getting weaker and weaker. In my mind . I thought that they sent me home to die. I was a mess. My sister went out to buy a pillow that sat up like a chair .I sat straight up for several days. I didn't want my lungs to collapse. I was so worried about that. I wasn't resting well. I had been listening to some gospel music, and reading my Bible. While I listen to Heaven 600 from the radio. I heard the psalmist sing songs of worship. As weak as I was. I kneeled down and prayed to GOD. I cried out. Lord help me! A song came on the radio, that said Lord I'm grateful by Gearldine Barkdale. I began to worship and praise GOD. Then I prayed some more. I read my Bible more and more. Then I prayed some more. This time something happened. It was different. It felt like GOD Himself came down from heaven and enter my body. My body Jerk, the tears rolled down my face. It felt like an electrical shocked. I started praises and thanking GOD. Then I walked slowly to my mother's room. I told her that GOD healed my body. " I said that I was praying to GOD and reading my Bible. It's like He came and put Himself inside of me. My mother was happy. I still could only breath but a little.

What I did next. First I stepped out on faith. I put down that breathing device that the doctor gave to me to breath through. I put that albuterol device down, and took small baby steps. I knew that I wasn't working alone. Each day I walk back and forth in the hallway. By faith, I felt myself getting stronger. I went from baby steps, to walking, to brisk walking in the hall way. Then I went from brisk walking , to walking up and down the stairs.

Next, I went from walking up and down the stairs to running. As I was walking by faith and not by sight. My appearance was terrible. My chest was giving me a little problem. It felt heavy , but that was alright.

My fiancé' came over. I drift off to sleep in his arms. I was awaken. I heard a voice say get up. I looked around . I saw no one again , I heard a voice say get up, and go back to that hospital. It was about 3:00a.m. in the morning. I went to my sister room and told her to go with me to the hospital. She get up and put her clothes on. I told my fiancé' that I will see him later. He went home to get ready for work.

We arrived at the hospital . I was being led by the Spirit. It was like someone was holding my hand guiding me where to go. We walked down a hall, then get on the elevator to the floor that I was on . I saw the nurse and the assistant that cared for me. As I walked over to the nurses station . I looked her in the eyes. "I said hi, do you remember me? As she looked up at me. The nurse stood up. I could see her with my spiritual eyes. I saw that she was afraid. In the spirit, she was backing up, and holding on to the chair. If one was to see her with their natural eyes. The nurse never moved. What I was seeing spiritual was her movement, reaction , and awe at me from the inside. I asked my sister . Do you see her? She's afraid of me. Why is she backing up?

My sister said , "I don't see anything." I asked her, you don't see what I see? So I looked over to the right, and I saw the nurse assistant. She looked back at me, but she was backing up. Again, " I asked my sister. Do you see her ? She's afraid too. I think that I was frightening my sister So I kept quite. My sister said since you are here. You probably want to go to the emergency room. You didn't get enough sleep. I agree with her, but I kept on talking about the Bible and GOD. We went to the emergency room and waited for the doctor. My sister called my mother and another sister of mine. She missed worked that day, and came to the emergency room where we were. I was given a room . I still continue to talk about GOD, the Bible, and Spiritual things. I talked about how GOD spoke to me, and told me to come here.

When the doctor came into the room. He asked what was going on? One of my sister spoke. She told the doctor, when I first got sick, that I was a patient her a couple of weeks ago . Then she told the doctor that I started reading my Bible constantly , and listening to gospel music. Then she told the doctor what I told her about GOD. Next thing I know the doctor took both of my sisters out into the hallway. I don't know what he told them. What I do know that I will not be going home any time soon.

It was noon time . More and more doctors were coming in the room to exam me. People were coming in the emergency room with all kind of sickness and complaints. That emergency room was over flowing with people. The more I stayed there in my room the Spirit was speaking to me. He said, majority of those people coming in are suffering with heart problems. As I listen to what the Spirit was speaking. I spoke, and repeated what was said. All those people coming in here are suffering with heart problems. My sister said . How do you know? I said the Spirit told me. They got quite. Then another doctor enter the room and asked, how was I doing?" I said good, but my chest hurt. Later on he sent in an I. V. therapist. He was ordered to give me a spinal tap. This man tried with all his might to put that needle in my back. He continue forcing that needle in my back. I was saying in the spirit. I am His sheep, I am His sheep, I am His sheep. The I.V therapist was getting upset. He spoke out. I can't get this needle to go through! People were still coming into the emergency room. I heard a lady yelled. My heart , my heart. Doctors were running through the hallway. They yelled out code blue, code blue. It was a lot going on . The I. V. therapist said. I am going to use one more needle. I need for you to be very still, please don't move. The needle did go through ,after many attempts. After the I.V. therapist left the room. A therapist enter the room. She asked me several questions. I answered the questions that she asked, then I went on talking about GOD. The therapist left the room , and said that she would be back. So we waited and waited. Three more doctors came in the room, and said that they were going to admitted me. So we agreed. Patiently I continue to wait with my sisters at my side. One of the doctors said that they were waiting for a floor to put me on. He stated that the emergency room was over crowded , and people are coming in complaining about their heart. "I said I know. He looked at me and left the room. A few hours later , the doctor said that they have a floor to put me on. My sister said alright. They waited with me until I left the emergency room. I told them that I am fine. Go home, because I am going to be alright.

I was taken to a floor that I never saw before. " I asked what kind of floor is this? A staff member said that it was for people with disorders. I looked at her as if something was wrong with her. I was given some kind of drug. I mind you as I said in the beginning. I wasn't resting well , and my chest hurt. They told me that I need some sleep. I took the pills, and thinking that I was going home the next day. When morning came . I felt like an alien from another planet. I looked as though I saw a ghost. My eyes was popping out of my head. I saw people looking strange. Glory Be to GOD. The Spirit of the Lord never left me. I continue to talk about God more. I was given pills, blood was drawn pressure taken frequently . When staff members were to give me medication , my body would feel strange. I called my family and told them that this place looked like a prison. I can't get out. My sister said What? I'm on my way. When she arrived. I looked as strange as the people in that place. They told her that I would be there for awhile, that I couldn't go home. I was so medicated that I couldn't write my own name. My sister was upset. She talked with one of the staff members. The staff member told my sister, make sure that you come to see her everyday . She stated that, when people are put here, family members forget about them, and that's what they like. It's a business, it's not about the people. My sister stated you don't have to worry about that, wrong sister wrong family. It was time for my sister to go home.

The next day two of my other sisters came along with my fiancé'. One of my sister, who is two year older than I, asked the doctors . Why do she looked like this? She looked like a zombie. When we brought her to the hospital she looked nothing like this. What did you do? What did you do?

Their response were. We gave her some medication to rest. As my sister yelled! What kind of medication ? They didn't want to tell her. Being the sister that she is. She demanded some answers. They told her. My sister said, don't give her anymore medication , and I will be looking into this situation believe that! My fiancé' was hot. He said I told ya'll not to give her anything. She came to the emergency room, and end up here ! The doctors said that it was best that they put me on that floor, because I was talking about GOD, aliens, and how GOD spoke to me. I was drug up, but I could still hear what was going on. My family left. I had to sit in classes that they gave to the patients. Yet the Spirit of GOD was still speaking to my spirit. His Spirit allowed me to listen in on conversation, while sitting across the room. As I blotted out to one of the staff assistant. How could you say that to this patient? When you have hidden secrets within yourself. I pulled him over to the side as the Spirit led me to asked him a question about himself. He looked as if he saw a ghost. I can't write down the question that I asked him, but his response was yes. I said, I know, and I told him to try Jesus. He node his head and went back to the table. So I sat back down. As my focus went over to the receptionist. The Spirit led me to ask this gentlemen a question? Who holds the power in His hands? He said President Clinton. I said no, GOD does. Then the receptionist said "Oh". Again I took a seat.

Later, some doctors came in to examine me in my room, then they left. I came out of my room, and took a seat away from the others. GOD anointed powers were all over me. I was being led by His Spirit. The outside of me was looking awful, but my inside was being renewed. As the day went by. More patients were brought to that floor. It looked like a drug business. The doctors were the dealers and the patients were the addicts.

They looked like zombies. As I sat back and watched. If a patient would talk out loud or one would express themselves. They would get punish. A staff member who happens to be a nurse, would give them a pill to shut them up. After receiving a pill. All the patient could do was to be quite, and fall asleep. It wasn't a place to send a person. Don't get me wrong. If a person feel that they can't handle situation , and need to see a doctor, so be it. I felt that we were being misunderstood, and needed a chance to be heard. Or could it be that they heard what they wanted to hear. Don't be so quick to rush. Look at the heart of a person. For me all it could have taken is just one. One that could have believe with me. If one person was spiritual. If one person knew their is a Creator. If one person had mercy for another. If one person believe their is a High Power. If one person believe that a person did hear from GOD. If one person had faith as small as a grain of mustard seed. If one person had wisdom and not just book knowledge of what they learned in school. If one person knew that mind, spirit, soul and body all goes together, and how God spoke everything into existence. If one person knew that GOD still chooses people. If one person would stand up and find another alterative, beside using medication. Maybe the Pharmaceutical companies wouldn't be so successful. So what do I do? No one was understanding me, but I know that the One who order me to go back to that hospital was listening. As I will this vessel before Him. I don't know what lies ahead for me. Only GOD Knows. Glory Be To GOD! He has the blueprints from beginning to the end. Yes I am still here in the hospital, and I continue to participate in the classes. The Spirit continue to give me revelation on the people who was around me. As I pulled them off to the side one by one. I said the Spirit told me to tell you this, and I would repeat it. I knew who was going home, before the patients and staff members. The staff members would look at me as if I was crazy. One of the staff member spoke out. "We didn't have any doctors ordered for that patient to go home. "I said, you don't know, but I do know who's going home. You guess it ! The Spirit was right. That person did go home. It was this lady there. She said that I am going home today. I told her no. I don't think so. I wasn't told anything about that. I do know that you will be here for awhile. She started yelling ! You don't know what you are talking about. I remain humble, and walk away. I remember walking towards my room, and I fell. There was nothing in my way. I just went down. Next thing I knew I opened up my mouth, and said. "Lord I surrender all to you." Please help me! The nurse came running over towards me. What happened? I said I fell. She gave me a cup of water, and took my pressure. It was time to eat dinner. I ate, shower, and went to bed.

As I drifted off to sleep. I felt my body sinking down into the bed. I said what's happening? Then I was trying to raise up, but I couldn't move. Something was happening. I saw my body still lying in the bed, but my spirit was taken out of the body. Only GOD knows what's going on. As I stood there looking at my body lying in the bed. My spirit was standing there glancing at me. Again, only GOD knows. Whether in the body, or out of the body . He knows all things. As GOD was showing me my life from a child to adult. I stood there and watch. GOD showed me things I've done in my life good and bad. Then I was shown water. As the Spirit led me by the hand. We were walking in the water. I continue to walk. The water came rushing. It was so much water. I thought that I was going to drown. I saw other people walking through the water behind me. A flood of water came rushing again. We all were drowning, but God lifted me out of the water. I heard screaming and yelling, then I heard nothing. I saw no more people. Then I was shown people in a building. Next, I heard loud screams and the building came falling down crushing the people. I saw fire everywhere. I fell on my knees in a praying position. I said to the LORD Father forgive me. As my spirit was out of the body . I don't know what was happening. Only God knows. I was told to stand up. So I stood up. As I glance over to the right. It was a rumbling sound. A fight broke out. The Beast was in rage, and a battle was going on. The Beast came after me, but an angel move in and protected me. A battle was taken place. I heard a roaring sound that of a lion. The Beast was coming a second time. He broke loose. I was putting up a fight. I mean I was fighting. Then the LORD stepped in. Again, a third time a rumbling sound. This went on for hours. Then I heard nothing, as the LORD reached out for my hand . I was frighten, I was fearful. I beg even more, because I heard what was being done. Then I was in another room. People were raising from graves. As I stood off with the LORD. The voice of the LORD spoke. I hold The Power. I asked the LORD this question? You are the GOD of who? And He showed me some colors . The colors were brown, black, yellow, white, red, of different nationality. Then He spoke. I Am the LORD of many. Then I asked the LORD to show me His face? The voice of the LORD spoke. You would not be able to handle it. I asked again? LORD show me your face ? Slowly as He turned around all I could see was a powerful bronzing light. I couldn't see a face. It blinded me. I put up my hands. " LORD I can't see. You are blinding me. The voice of the LORD spoke. I told you that you couldn't handle it. Then I heard these trumpet sounds. It would not stop. The LORD spoke again. I Am the Alpha the Omega the First and the Last the Beginning and the End. I Am GOD. Then the earth opened, as it was being swallowed up, and everything was gone. Then in the spirit. I saw a new beginning. I saw a newness, flowers, gardens, trees, freshness. Like a new earth nothing being tainted. Then my spirit went back in my body. As I raised up . I screamed and yelled. I felt like I have been beaten down. My body was hurting and sore. I was afraid, and "I said what was that? Who do I tell? I dare not to speak. If I tell someone, they wouldn't understand, because I didn't understood. If I speak out on this, then they really would think that I am crazy. As a staff member came running to my room and opened the door. Are you alright? We heard you yelling and screaming. I told him that I was fine. I knew something took place that night, and I was different.

As I still remained a patient. I knew that I was being changed, renewed, and born again. I really put the name of Jesus in my mouth. The LORD was giving me revelation, while still being a patient.

He was directing me to tell other patients who was ready to go home, about their condition , and who was being bound with strong holds. All I could do was to be obedient, and will myself before Him. He choose me I didn't choose Him. After hearing His voice and seeing His Power.

I reverence Him even more. The doctor did give me some medication after staying one week in the hospital. I was able to go home. Yet I had some medicine in my system, with GOD in my heart . Yashua Jesus name on my lips, and the precious Holy Spirit inside.

The second day that I was home . I had a glass of water and the prescribe medication in my hand . I was ready to take a pill. I heard the voice of The LORD spoke . There is nothing wrong with you. Don't take another one of those pills. "I knew it!", "I knew it !". I picked up the telephone, and called my mother . I told her what just happened again I shouted "I knew it , I knew it!" . There was nothing wrong with me. The Spirit of the LORD told me to stop taking those pills. I am alright. My mother agreed with me, and she said I've been praying . They should have never given you anything to begin with. I threw some of those pills in the trash can. I kept a few pills in the bottle, because I had an appointment to see this therapist. A week went by. It was time to go and to see this therapist. As I enter his room. He said have a seat. So I sat down, and he asked me this question. When you turn your television on, do you see people talking to you ? As I pretended to go along with him, and acting like I was still taking the prescribe medication. I answered yes doctor and why is that? His answer was good, then the pills are working. I stood up, and said "Sir you should be ashamed of yourself! How could you people be so insensitive? I stood up, said thanks, but no thanks. I told him to take these pills and keep them for himself, because you need them more than I do . As I was walking toward the door. "I said, and another thing, this is my first and last visit . I told him, " Oh sir , don't forget to make yourself an appointment." The devil is a liar. I walk out of that room as a proud child of GOD. I never took another pill or had another therapist visit . The LORD, Yashua Jesus, and the Spirit, were all I needed, and they are my everything.

Now I am able to walk again, breath again, sleep in in my bed lying flat down . To Yahweh Be The Glory ! What I would like to say to the readers and believers . Always trust your instance. If you know deep down in your heart , that you had an encounter with your Maker. Stand on that Truth . If GOD has spoken revelation to you, even though you didn't understood . Stand on that Truth. If GOD spoken life back into you . Stand on that Truth. If no one believe you, but GOD .Stand on that Truth. If you heard the voice of Authority. Stand on that Truth. If you know that GOD created us and He knows His children from beginning to end . Stand on that Truth. I say trust and believe Him. GOD is the Only One who sees and know our purpose, destiny, plan, and future . If anyone every calls you crazy. "You say yes!" I'm crazy for Jesus . If we are out of our mind, it is for the sake of GOD, If we are In our right mind it is for you. (2 Corinthians 5:13)

Believe It!!!!!!!!!!!!!!!!!!!!!!

Appendix - Key Points

Reconciliation

Do you know what it means to be reconciled to God ?
2 Corinthians 5:18-21 ....For God was in Christ , reconciling the world to Himself , no longer counting people's sins against them . This is the wonderful message He has given us to tell others ...

Ephesians 2:11-21 ...Though you once were far away from God , now you have been brought near to Him because of the blood of Christ .
Reconciliation begins with a recognition that without Christ we are lost and separated from God .

Romans 5:1-2 Therefore, since we have been made right in God's sight by faith , we have peace with God ..
Reconciliation with God comes through faith and brings peace.

Repentance

Is repentance necessary ?
Ezekiel 33:10-16...The good works of righteous will not save them if they turn to sin nor will the sins of evil people destroy them if they repent and turn from their sins..
Repentance leads to forgiveness of sin .

Jeremiah 5:3...They are determined ,with faces set like stone ; they have refused to repent . The unrepentant heart rejects God and remains in sin's grasp .

Luke 13:1-8...And you will also perish unless you turn from evil ways and turn to God . Jesus taught that without repentance we face judgment .

Luke 15:10 ...There is joy in the presence of God's angels when even one sinner repents . All heaven rejoices when one sinner repents.

What is repentance ?

Mathew 3:1-3 …Turn from your sins and turn to God …
Repentance means being sorry for sin and being committed to a new way of life , serving God .

Luke 19:8 Zacchaeus ..Said to the Lord , .. If I have overcharged people on their taxes , I will give them back four times as much !
Repentance is made complete by changed behavior .

Exodus 9:27-34 …When Pharoah saw this , he refusing his official sinned yet again by stubbornly refusing to do as they had promised …
Repentance that produces no lasting change is insincere.

Is repentance one-time only, or do we need to repent over And over when we sin?

Psalm 51:16-17 … The sacrifice you want is a broken spirit . A broken and repentant heart , O God , you will not despise .
While salvation is a one –time event , God is pleased by broken and contrite hearts willing to confess and repent of sin .

1John 1:8-9 …If we say we have no sin , we are refusing to accept the truth . But if we confess our sins to Him ..
Confession and repentance of sin are constant mark of the person walking in the light of fellowship with God .

PROMISE FROM GOD: Acts 2:38 Each of you must turn from your sins and turn to God and be baptized in the name of Yashua Jesus the Christ for forgiveness of your sins . Then you will receive the gift of the Holy Spirit .

Salvation
Do you know what it means to be saved?

Romans 4:4-8 …What a joy for those whose sin is no longer counted against them by the Lord .

Romans 3:24 …Yet now God is His gracious kindness declares us not guilty .
Being saved means no longer having our sins count against us but rather being forgiven by the grace of God .

Psalm 103:11-12 …Remove the stain of my guilt . Create in me a clean heart , O God .. Being saved means the stain of guilt has been washed away .

1Peter 2:9-10 … Once you received none of God's mercy; now you have received His mercy .

Romans 3:21-24 … He has done this through Christ , who has feed us by taking away our sins .
Being saved means we are forgiven in Christ .

How can we be saved?
Romans 10:13 …Anyone who calls on the name of the Lord will be saved .
God's Word promise salvation to anyone who calls on Yashua Jesus' name .
John 3:16 …For God so loved the world that He gave His only Son , so that everyone who believes in Him will not perish but have eternal life.

John 5:24 …I assure you , those who listen to my message and believe in God who sent me have eternal life .
Yashua Jesus Himself promised that those who believe in Him will be saved .

Is salvation available to anyone ?
Luke 2:11-12 … The Savior ---Yes , the Messiah , the Lord has been born tonight in Bethlehem . Yashua Jesus was born in a humble stable among very ordinary people to powerfully demonstrate that salvation is available to anyone who sincerely seeks Him .

Revelation 20:11-21 :3 … And the dead were judged according to the things written in the books ..
Salvation is available to all , but a time will come when it will be too late to receive it.

How can I be sure of my salvation?
1 Peter 1:5 And God , in His mighty power , will protect you until you receive this salvation ..
Salvation brings the sure hope of eternal life .

Romans 8:12 – 17 ... For all who are led by the Holy Spirit are children of God
.

The Holy Spirit takes up residence in our hearts and assures us we are God's
children .

Mathew 14:23-33 ..."Save me , Lord!" he shouted . Instantly Jesus reached out
His hand and grabbed him .
We cannot save ourselves from sin , guilt , judgment , and spiritual death . Only
Yashua Jesus Christ can save us .

PROMISE FROM GOD
Romans 10:9 ...For if you confess with your mouth that Yashua Jesus is Lord and
believe in your heart that God raised Him from the dead , you will be saved .

Songs To Him In The Tabernacle

SONGS TO HIM IN THE TABERNACLE

REVELATION 21:3 And I heard a great voice out of Heaven saying, Behold, the tabernacle of God is with men, and He will dwell with them And they shall be His people, and God Himself shall be with them and Be their God.

BE STILL

Be Still

Open up your heart
Open up your ears
Open up your eyes
Open up your mouth
And invite Him in

Be Still
Open up your heart
Open up your ears
Open up your eyes
Open up your mouth
And invite Him in

Know that He is God
Know Him for yourself
He want to have a
Personal relationship with you

Be Still

Open up your heart
Open up your ears
Open up your eyes
Open up your mouth
And invite Him in

Be Still

Open up your heart
Open up your ears
Open up your eyes
Open up your mouth
And invite Him in

Be Still

Know that He is God

Be Still
Be Still
Be Still

For He is God

Be Still
Be Still
Be Still

For He is God

Be Still
Be Still
Be Still

Change

When Jesus walked into my life
The first thing He showed me
What I had to change.

I had to change me
Look inside myself
Are you satisfy

Be true to yourself
You don't have to lie
Get real Be honest
Meditate on Me

Be still and know that I Am God
Be still and know that I Am God

He showed me
What I had to do
Get real Be honest

When Jesus walked into my life
The first thing
He showed me
What I had to change
I had to change me

Look inside myself
Am I please with myself
Am I true to myself
Do I love myself

If the answer is yes
Then you can love Me

If the answer is no
Leave your request with Me

Do as I told you to do
Change you

Look inside of yourself
Get real Be honest

Be still and know that I Am God
Be still and know that I Am God

The answers are inside of you
You know what to do
Change you

Dreams

Jeremiah 29:11 For I know the plans I have for you. "Declares the LORD," plans to prosper you and not to harm you, plans to give you hope and a future.

DREAMS

Dream Big, Dream dream
You all have a
Dream living right inside of you
You dream
I dream
We dream
They dream
The greatest gift
Live right inside of you
Let your dream
Become a reality
Dream, Dream
Dream Big
Never let no one tell you
Not to dream
Dream Dream
Dream Big
God put a dream
Right inside of you
Release that dream
That he deposit
Right inside of you
Dream Dream
Dream Big
Bigger than you ever
Could imagine
Dream Dream
Dream Big, Bigger than you can ever imagine.

FAITH

F.A.I.T.H
Faith
Faith
Faith

Faith is the substance of things hope for
The evidence of things not seen

When God say do it
Just do it
Do it

F.A.I.T.H
Faith
Faith
Faith

Faith is the substance of things hope for
The evidence of things not seen

F.A.I.T.H
Faith
Faith
Faith

You have faith
I have faith
We have faith

Trust and believe
Whatever Jesus say
Just do it
Do it
Do it

Trust and believe
Whatever God say
Just do it
Do it
Do it

You have faith
I have faith
We have faith

Trust and believe
Whatever Jesus say
Just do it
Do it
Do it

You have faith
I have faith
We have faith

Whatever God say
Just do it
Do it
Do it

F.A.I.T.H
Faith
Faith
Faith

His Faithfulness

His faithfulness will be your shield and rampart

He who dwells in the shelter of the Most High
Will rest in the shadow of the Almighty

His faithfulness will be your shield and rampart

I will say of the Lord, He is my refuge and fortress
My God, in whom I trust

His faithfulness will be your shield and rampart

Surely He will save you from the fowlers snare
And from the deadly pestilence

His faithfulness will be your shield and rampart

He will cover you with His feathers
And under His wings you will find refuge

His faithfulness will be your shield and rampart

You will not fear the terror of night
Nor the arrow that flies by day

His faithfulness will be your shield and rampart

Nor the pestilence that stalks in the darkness
Nor the plague that destroys at midday

His faithfulness will be your shield and rampart

A thousand my fall at your side
Ten thousand at your right hand
But it will not come near you

His faithfulness will be your shield and rampart

I am THAT I am

I am that I am
That's who you are
Jesus is in His Father
You are in Jesus
Jesus is in you

So you say
I am that I am
That's who you are

If you have seen Jesus
You have seen the Father
You are in Jesus
Jesus is in you

So you say
I am that I am
That's who you are

Be still before the Lord
All mankind, He has roused
Himself from His holy dwelling

Jesus in is His Father   .
You are in Jesus
Jesus is in you

So you say
I am that I am
That's who you are

If you heard of Jesus
You heard of the Father
Jesus is in you
You are in Jesus

So you say
I am that I am ,that's who you are.

Jehovah

Oh my Jehovah Jireh
Jehovah Nissi
Jehovah Shalom

The Alpha and Omega
The Beginning
The End
The First
The Last
You are God

As I heed
To Your call
You are my
All and All

The Alpha and Omega
The Beginning
The End
The First
The Last
You are God

You chose me
To be Your instrument
You are my
All and All

LORD God
I give You
My all and all

Oh my Jehovah
My Jehovah
My Jehovah

You are God

Oh my
Jehovah
Jehovah Jireh
Jehovah Nissi
Jehovah Shalom

You are God

The Alpha and Omega
The Beginning
The End
The First
The Last
You are God
I give You
My all and all

Oh my Jehovah
My Jehovah Jireh
Jehovah Nissi
Jehovah Shalom

You are God
Oh my Jehovah
You are God
Oh my Jehovah
You are God

Oh my Jehovah
My Jehovah Jireh
Jehovah Nissi
Jehovah Shalom

You are God

The Voice

Man up
I say stand up
The women are calling

Jeremiah
Tommy
Charles
Ezra
Paul
Daniel
Robert

Where did you go?
Did you loose your position?

Man up
I say stand up
The women are calling

George
Harry
Michael
Jonathan
Chris
Wayne
Richard

Get back in line
You are the head
Know your position
Love your wife
As Christ love the church
And gave Himself up for the church
The more you love her
You won't disappoint her

Man up
I say stand up
The women are calling

Peter
John
William
James
Al
Sean
Calvin

Come back
The family needs you
All that wasted time
You spend with your friends
You could give it to your sons

Man up
I say stand up
The women are calling

Bruce
Raymond
Marcus
Brandon
Ronnie
Justin
David

Go back
To your love one's
Your daughters need you too
Teach them
Love them
Like you love your extra curriculum

Man up
I say stand up
The women are calling
Lee
Andrew
Dexter
Alex
Joe
Floyd
Thaddeus

Work it out
Stay there
Love the family
Keep people out of your ear
And your space
Do some research
See if they have it all together
If not guard your ears

Man up
I say stand up
The women are calling

Lewis
Thomas
Terrell
Jimmy
Brian
Tyrone
Victor

Go back to your position
Follow the pattern
That God has created
God the head and Father
Jesus the son
Spirit the gift of God

That's who you are
Now, that's where you come from
You are made in His image
And so are your

Wife
Sons and daughters
Man up
I say stand up
The women are calling

Get your family
Back in order
For those name that are not written
You know who you are
Make Your Creator proud of you
And your families .
Get back into position
God has many treasures
That He wants to release
So stand up
Then you can man up
Get back into position

Man Up

Man up
Stand up
The women are calling

Man up
Stand up
The women are calling

Man up stand up
Your sons and daughters
They need you

Man up stand up
Your sons and daughters
They need you

Where did you go?
You lost your position
Go back
Get in line
Know your position
It ain't hard
It too easy

Man up
Stand up
The women are calling

Man up
Stand up
The women are calling

Man up
Your sons and daughters
They need you

Man up
Your sons and daughters
They need you

Go back to them
Teach them
Love them
Respect them
Praise them

Man up
Stand up
The women are calling

Man up
Stand up
The women are calling

Man up
Your sons and daughters
They need you

Man up
Your sons and daughters
They need you

MY GRACE

My grace is sufficient
My grace is sufficient

He said
My grace is sufficient
But LORD
Take this pain away

My grace is sufficient

What will the people say

My grace is sufficient

But LORD
Why do it have to be this way

My grace is sufficient

If I take this thorn away
You would go back
Doing the same thing

I number the hairs of hair
On your head
I see everything
I had to humble you
Your pride came before the fall
Your tongue was so boastful
It was necessary
To do what I had to do

My grace is sufficient

Your ego became bigger
Than you

My grace is sufficient
That thorn that I planted in you
This will keep you on
The straight and narrow
Remember I chose you
You are my instrument

My grace is sufficient
My grace is sufficient

When you lift up praises
You will always
Remember Me

My grace is sufficient
My grace is sufficient

Praises

Praise Him
Praise Him
Praise the Lord

May the praise of God
Be in your mouth

Praise the Lord
Praise Him with the sound of the trumpet

Praise Him with tambourine and dancing
Let everything that has breath praise the Lord.

Praise Him
Praise Him
Praise the Lord

From the lips of children and infants
You have ordained praise
I will extol the Lord at all times
His praise will always be on my lips

Hosanna , Hosanna to the Son of David
We love You we praise You
From the lips of children and infants
You have ordained praise

Hosanna, Hosanna to the Son of David
We love You, we praise You
Praise Him
Praise the Lord
To the Son of David
We love You
We praise You

Hosanna, Hosanna to the Son of David
We love You, we praise You.

Return To He

R-E-P-E-N-T
R-E-P-E-N-T
R-E-P-E-N-T

Repent
And return to He
R-E-P-E-N-T
Repent
And return to He
He will make you free

Come
My children
Return to He

Come
My children
Return to He

Repent
He will make you free

R-E-P-E-N-T
R-E-P-E-N-T
R-E-P-E-N-T

Repent
And return to He

R-E-P-E-N-T

Repent
And return to He
He will make you free

R-E-P-E-N-T
Repent
And return to He

Come my children
Return to He
Come my children
Return to He
He will make you free

It's easy
As 1,2,3
Come my children
Return to He
He will make you free

Come
And repent to He

It's easy
As 1,2, 3

Come
And return to He
He will make you free
Come my children
Return to He

It's easy
As 1,2, 3

Come
And repent to He

It's easy
As 1,2, 3
Repent
And return to He

Salt And Light

Salt and Light of the world
That's who we are
Salt and Light of the world
That's who we are

If we lost our salt-ness
Then we are worth-less
We have to be about
Our Lord business
So let us go and be a witness

Salt and Light of the world
That's who we are
Salt and Light of the world
That's who we are

We go out into the world
Two by two
That means me and you
Let your light shine from within
So they can see the Christ in we

Salt and Light of the world
That's who we are
Salt and Light of the world
That's who we are

So don't lose your salt-ness
Keep yourself
Fill with His Holy Word
So they can see the Christ in we

Salt and Light of the world
That's who we are
Salt and Light of the world
That's who we are

Amen! He's Coming Soon

The grace of the Lord Jesus be with
God's people
Amen
The grace of the Lord Jesus be with
God's people
Amen
Yes, He's coming soon
Amen
Yes, He's coming soon
Amen

Blessed are those who wash their robes
Amen
That they may have the right to the tree of life
Amen
May you go through the gates into the City
Amen

The grace of the Lord Jesus be with
God's people
Amen
The grace of the Lord Jesus be with
God's people
Amen

The Spirit and the Bride say
"Come"
Let him that hear say
"Come"
Who ever is thirsty say
"Come"
Let him take the free gift of life
"Come"

The grace of the Lord Jesus be with
God's people

Amen
The grace of the Lord Jesus be with
God's people
Amen

He's coming real soon
Amen
He's coming real soon
Amen
Let him take the free gift of water of life
Amen
He's coming soon
Amen

ABBA

Some call him the
God of Abraham
God of Isaac
God of Jacob
I call Him Abba
Abba
Because He has been so good to me.
So good that He held nothing
Back from me that He saw fit for me.
Though at times it may have been ruff.
For Abba knew that I could handle it.
He prepared me for such a time as this.
When Abba came and spoke these words
I am the Alpha and Omega
The First and Last
The Beginning and the End
I am God
For he has spoken
Some call Him the
God of Abraham
God of Isaac
God of Jacob
I call Him Abba
Abba because He brought Revelation to me
He showed me a tiny bit of Heaven
He breathe the breath of Life back in me
He raised up a warrior
And showed me how
To fight the enemy
Some call him the
God of Abraham
God of Isaac
God of Jacob
I call Him Abba
Abba
As he tried me through the fire

Like the three Hebrews in the lions den
I came out without a snitch
He saw that I was a warrior
For I was ready for the day of battle
Some call Him the
God of Abraham
God of Isaac
God of Jacob
I call Him Abba
Abba
Because He told me to sound the alarm
He called me one of his messengers
He gave me an assignment
To sound the alarm:
The alarm has now been sounded
He saw that I was equipped
As I will myself before Him
I heeded to His call
Some call Him the
God of Abraham
God of Isaac
God of Jacob
I call Him Abba
Who is my Father
I call Him Abba
Who is my Father
I call Him Abba

MY GRACE

My grace is sufficient
My grace is sufficient

He said
My grace is sufficient
But LORD
Take this pain away

My grace is sufficient

What will the people say

My grace is sufficient

But LORD
Why do it have to be this way

My grace is sufficient

If I take this thorn away
You would go back
Doing the same thing

I number the hairs of hair
On your head
I see everything
I had to humble you
Your pride came before the fall
Your tongue was so boastful
It was necessary
To do what I had to do

My grace is sufficient

Your ego became bigger
Than you

My grace is sufficient
That thorn that I planted in you
This will keep you on
The straight and narrow
Remember I chose you
You are my instrument

My grace is sufficient
My grace is sufficient

When you lift up praises
You will always
Remember Me

My grace is sufficient
My grace is sufficient

Touched By Him

Jacob for you wrestle with God
You wouldn't let go
You wouldn't let go

Jacob for you struggle with God
You wrestle with Him
Until day break
The angel saw that, he could not over power you
He touched the socket of your hip.

Jacob for you wrestle with God
You wouldn't let go
You wouldn't let go

Jacob for you wrestle with God
You wouldn't let go
You wouldn't let go

"Jacob, angel asked you to let go
You said I will not let go
Until You bless me.
Jacob wrestle with God
Until day break
Jacob saw God face to face
He asked you what is your name?

Jacob for you wrestle with God
You wrestle with God
You wouldn't let go
You wouldn't let go

He asked you what is your name?
"Jacob, you answered
He answered back
This is what He said
Your name will no longer

Be Jacob but Israel

For you have struggle with God
And with men
For you have overcome

Jacob you wrestle with God
You wrestle with God
You wouldn't let go
You wouldn't let go

Jacob you wrestle with God
You wrestle with God
You wouldn't let go
You wouldn't let go

God answered
Your name will no longer
Be Jacob but Israel
Israel
Israel
Israel
For you wrestle with God
And with men
For you have overcome
You wouldn't let go
You wouldn't let go

INVITATION TO THE FAMILY

GREETING,

To the family, that include everyone. If you are Still breathing, that means you too. I pray that I will see you all in heaven. If you are out of fellowship with GOD, and Yashua Jesus. I pray that you get Yourself back in line and develop a personal relationship with them. Family Do pray for the Holy Spirit. He is your teacher. He is a gift from GOD. Open Up your mouth and heart and invite Him in. GOD, Yashua Jesus, and the Holy Spirit are waiting. It's not hard. The same way you chose the company You keep, is the same way you can choose GOD, Yashua Jesus, and the Holy Spirit. They are a Union. All three are **One**. So family love your Neighbors as the Messiah and GOD love you. Put away all trivial nonsense. Your life is so much important than that. Do focus on where you want to Spend Eternity. May your work you done on earth speak for you in this life. Then you could look forward to spending your life in the next life. There is Life after death. So seek Him, while He is still to be found. Do know it's Never about you. It is all about Him, and what He did for us on the cross. Get back in fellowship with the Lord. If you don't know who He is. Go and Purchase yourself a Bible. Right their your relationship with your Maker and Creator will develop. Ask me how I know? Because He did it for Me. Then partner up with a man or woman of GOD who know the Word of GOD, who are living by His Word, and walking by faith. Fellowship with Believers in the Messiah at a Tabernacle. Where your spirit are feed and Lifted. So family love your neighbors as yourself. I Pray that you will Accept my invitation . I pray that I get to meet you all in heaven. GOD first love you so love Him back.

Where the **Spirit** of the **Lord** is,
There is **freedom**.